TRADER JON'S

ALSO BY JAMES L. DICKERSON

Colonel Tom Parker
The Curious Life of Elvis Presley's Eccentric Manager

Chips Moman
The Record Producer Whose Genius Changed American Music

Living on Deadline
The Amazing Adventures of a Southern Journalist

Faith Hill
The Long Road Back

That's Alright, Elvis
The Untold Story of Elvis's First Guitarist
and Manager, Scotty Moore

Just for a Thrill
Lil Hardin Armstrong, First Lady of Jazz

Ashley Judd
Crying on the Inside

Devil's Sanctuary
An Eyewitness History of Mississippi Hate Crimes
(with Alex A. Alston Jr.)

Mojo Triangle:
Birthplace of Country, Blues, Jazz and Rock 'n' Roll

Legend of the Soul Eater (novel)

Love on the Rocks: Romance to the Rescue (novel)

TRADER JON'S

Cradle of U.S. Naval Aviation

JAMES L. DICKERSON

With photographs by

Steve Gardner

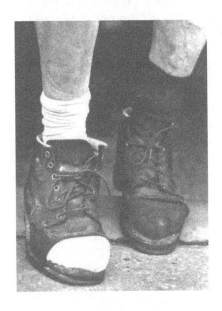

SARTORIS
LITERARY
GROUP

Sartoris Literary Group, Inc.
Jackson, Mississippi
www.sartorisliterary.com

We dedicate this book to the late Trader Jon, whose real name was Martin Weissman; his wife Jackii, their two children Dahn and Cheri; to all the Blue Angels pilots who frequented the bar, the wilderness man who simply went by the name Tex, the late cartoonist Jeff MacNelly, the newspaperman man who allowed us to publish his poem about Trader Jon's only on condition of anonymity, the U.S. Navy, the thousands of customers who sought refuge in the bar, and, of course, the dancers who shared their stories with us: Cookie, Julie, Krystal, Lisa, and Rive.

TRADER JON'S

CONTENTS

"I have my own world here.

Outside the door, it's different.

In here, it's just . . . well, good."

—Trader Jon

Blue Angels doing what they do best.   istockphoto.com

1

PENSACOLA, FLORIDA

July 1976

Blue Angels, Thunderbirds Initiated

In the dim light of the banquet room, 650 pair of wing-weary eyes shone bright as stars on a moonless night. Music filled the smoky air, a tribute to Bicentennial America, the world's first true democracy.

America the bee-you-tee-full!

Singing at the tops of their voices, the United States Naval and Air Force cadets sat clustered around a rickety table, elbow to elbow. A single light soft-focused a red halo on a one-foot-high stage on which the United States Naval Cadet Choir stood in neat rows, spit-polished to perfection.

Cigarette smoke, spiked with the odor of warm beer, floated like cotton candy clouds in and out of the red glow. On the walls of the vast room were hand-painted murals, adventuresome scenes taken from the postcards of France, Portugal and Great Britain, pictures painted by a country girl from Dothan, Alabama.

In the dark that clung to the walls like a protective cloak, the murals remained largely unnoticed, pristine fantasies of an artist with an eye for the surreal. In the audience were two of America's heroes of the Space Age—Astronauts Deke Slayton and Alan Shepard, the first American to travel in space. Surrounding them were hundreds of former and current members of the Blue Angels and the Thunderbirds, the well-publicized Air Force and Navy precision flying teams.

The Blue Angels, which are based in Pensacola, were formed in 1946 by Admiral Chester Nimitz, Chief of Naval Operations, to raise public interest in the Navy precision flying team—and to boost Navy morale. In total, seventeen officers voluntarily serve with the Blue Angels. Every year the team selects three tactical jet pilots to relieve departing members.

The Blue Angels commanding officer is selected each year by the Chief of Naval Operations. Always referred to as the "Boss," he flies the Number 1 jet. This year the Boss was a Top Gun named CDS Casey Jones.

With the blessings of the Pentagon, everyone there that night had been flown for that most sacred of all paramilitary events—the initiation of the Nubies. The fact that it was the Bicentennial made the celebration all that much more special.

The 1976 Blue Angels Team.

CDR Casey Jones, Boss	LT Al Cisneros		LT John Miller	Capt Phil Brooks
LCDR Leo Boor	Capt Bill Holverstott		LT John Patton	Capt Steve Petit
Maj Steve Murray	LT Denny Sapp		LT Mike Deeter	LTJG Al Pulley
LCDR Tim Peterson	LT Jim Bauer		LT Nile Kraft	

For Shepard and Slayton, who in 1975 was one of three American astronauts to participate in the first United States-Soviet Union joint space mission, it was a reunion with special memories. Sent to the Pensacola Naval Air Station in the late 1950s and early 1960s for special training, Shepard and Slayton—along with all the other original Mercury 7 astronauts—had found comfort at Trader Jon's in times of extraordinary stress.

In this room and in the adjoining room, where women danced topless and men sat in the dark to bathe their sorrows in one-ounce

Trader Jon

shots of whisky, gin and scotch, hard-fought battles were won or lost at the toss of a furtive glance.

Trader Jon's—home away from home for the Pensacola-based Blue Angels and their first cousins, the Thunderbirds. And, of course, America's space-age heroes, the astronauts. But whatever the thoughts going through their minds, they kept them to themselves. Tonight was Nubie night, when new recruits for the Blues and the Thunderbirds were to be initiated.

On stage were the squadron commanders for each eight-member team. With that sense of camaraderie that flyers alone possess, and that can never truly be understood by non-flyers, the two men embraced and then exchanged the gifts they had clutched, out of sight, behind their backs.

As the room erupted into wild applause and cheers, the squadron commanders called up their second in command, followed in time by the third in command, and so on, until all sixteen members of the flying team—including the newly-initiated Newbies—were on stage, all of them hugging and hooting, exchanging gifts.

With microphone in hand, Trader Jon himself—the only man in the nation to ever have a Navy airfield named in his honor—ambled onstage to wish the flyers well.

"Bee-you--too-full," purred the little man with the big smile.

And when the flyers departed in the wee hours—the Blue Angels in their supercharged A-4s, and the Thunderbirds in their T-38

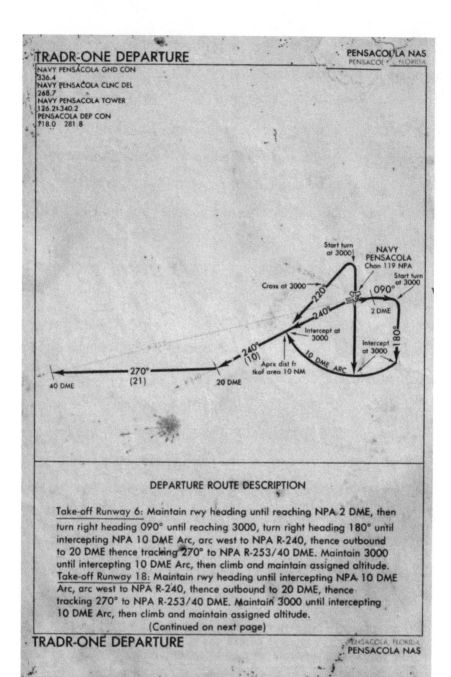

TRADR-ONE DEPARTURE

PENSACOLA NAS
PENSACOLA FLORIDA

NAVY PENSACOLA GND CON
336.4
NAVY PENSACOLA CLNC DEL
268.7
NAVY PENSACOLA TOWER
126.2 340.2
PENSACOLA DEP CON
118.0 281.8

DEPARTURE ROUTE DESCRIPTION

Take-off Runway 6: Maintain rwy heading until reaching NPA 2 DME, then turn right heading 090° until reaching 3000, turn right heading 180° until intercepting NPA 10 DME Arc, arc west to NPA R-240, thence outbound to 20 DME thence tracking 270° to NPA R-253/40 DME. Maintain 3000 until intercepting 10 DME Arc, then climb and maintain assigned altitude.
Take-off Runway 18: Maintain rwy heading until intercepting NPA 10 DME Arc, arc west to NPA R-240, thence outbound to 20 DME, thence tracking 270° to NPA R-253/40 DME. Maintain 3000 until intercepting 10 DME Arc, then climb and maintain assigned altitude.

(Continued on next page)

TRADR-ONE DEPARTURE

PENSACOLA, FLORIDA
PENSACOLA NAS

Talons—they left on the only U.S. Navy runway named after a mortal man. TRADR-ONE DEPARTURE reads the route description. Take-off runways six, eighteen, twenty-four and twenty-six . . . Varoooooom.

Moments after takeoff, the jets thundered one hundred feet above Palafox Street, clearly in violation of the law, dipping their wings in tribute to the man who has done more for naval aviation than all the Top Guns, chiefs and commanders combined—Trader Jon.

Trader Jon, coming and going.

2

IN THE BEGINNING

Born in 1914 in New York City, Trader Jon didn't get where he is today by attaching himself to anyone's coattails. He did it with hard work, and by mastering the ancient art of exaltation. Trader knows how to make almost anyone feel important. It is the key to his success. That knowledge arrived early in life. By the age of twelve, he was making it on his own, peddling ice cream along the people-infested beaches of New York.

"I did such a good job I was handed a concession, where I was the boss," he explains, halfway laughing. "By then, I was selling ice cream to the other peddlers."

Pushing ice cream was only a four months a year proposition, but always he saved what he earned, so that by the time he was sixteen, he had enough money tucked away to pursue his dream to leave home and travel. From New York, he went to California, where he worked at various jobs until he was old enough to open a bar of his own at the age of twenty-one. Then it was on to Nevada, Miami, Key West, and, finally, Pensacola.

When Trader arrived in Pensacola in 1953, it was a city in transition. For many years, home of one of the greatest fishing fleets in America, ships by the thousands sailed out of the port in search of snapper. All that came to an end, however, by the time World War II broke out. In the years immediately following the war, Pensacola hung up its fishnets and became a military town—home of the Pensacola Naval Air Station.

Yet, still there was a tradition to carry on.

When Pensacola was known as the Snapper Capital of the World, fishing fleets from ports stretching all the way up to New England and then across the Atlantic to Norway, left home in search of the friendly climate and fertile snapper grounds that lay offshore from Pensacola.

What resulted was a hodgepodge of Southerners, New Englanders, and a host of immigrants from all over the world who fished the same waters, loved the same women—and let off steam in the same waterfront bars. That was the beginning of the wide-open, anything goes reputation of Palafox Street.

In the old days, Pensacola was known as a Hangover Port. As if to officially sanction that reputation, the city set up special "public

Trader Jon

Historic Palafox Street refurbished to its former glory   istockphoto.com

drunk" fines. The regular fine was ten dollars, but fishermen paid only five dollars. At the turn of the century, boat captains, always in the market for a good crew, loaded up horse-drawn wagons with iced beer and drove them slowly down Palafox Street early in the mornings. Hung over, rubber-legged sailors flocked to the wagon, sampling the beer as the wagon crept back toward the ship. By the time the wagon arrived, the would-be sailors were so shaky they were grateful when the captain offered them a place aboard ship to stretch out and sober up. When the sailors awoke, the ship already was far out to sea.

Those days are gone now, but the tradition—operating under somewhat modified circumstances—lives on. What Trader found when he arrived in Pensacola was a port filled with wet-behind-the-ears naval cadets, many away from home for the first time. Others were part of the seasoned stable that is always part of any port, naval or air.

"There were thousands of those kids here," Trader says. "They were the start of my business."

In the beginning, there wasn't much to Trader Jon's: a hole-in-the-wall where thirsty sailors could come in out of the hot sun and drink their fill of rum or beer. It was a bar like any other. In order to have something to cover the bare walls, Trader encouraged his customers to bring items in to trade for their drinks. Word spread.

Soon Trader was swamped with artifacts. Some of the items were little more than junk; others were steeped in history and tradition. Some of those early trades still count among his best. For example, there is a ship's portal mounted on the wall directly behind the bar. The portal was salvaged from a nineteenth century four-mast schooner. It is very valuable.

Still, even after offering to trade drinks for artifacts, Trader was only treading water economically. Then, in the years between 1958 and 1960, three things happened that forever changed his life. First, while touring the farm country of southern Alabama, near Dothan, he met a country girl named Jackii. Soon they were married and his young bride—who fancied herself an artist—persuaded Trader to sponsor Pensacola's first street art exhibit. Secondly, Trader began hiring strippers to work in the bar, local women, who for a nominal fee, would take off their clothes in the amber glow of a passion light, and talk shop with the sailors between performances. And thirdly, Trader adopted the trademark that has stuck with him all these years—mismatched socks.

"I was invited to a ship's party," he explains. "It was a costume party, so I dressed as a port-starboard. I wore one red sock and one green sock. That meant that I was coming and going at the same time."

Trader knew right away that he had found his niche: he won first prize at the party and a check for one hundred dollars.

Since those early days, the list of people who have passed through Trader's doors and left mementos resembles a who's who of American pop culture: near the cash register is a ship's bell left by French oceanographer Jacques-Yves Cousteau; at the rear of the bar is a saddle left by actor John Wayne—and pictures left by countless squadrons of Navy pilots, movie actors, writers, political cartoonists and politicians.

Once, England's Prince Andrew—the kid brother of Prince Charles and second in line to the crown—visited Pensacola as a student crew member aboard Her Majesty's Ship Hermes. While in Pensacola, the twenty-year-old prince made several pilgrimages to Trader's, creating quite a stir among the city's socialites, who felt that the bar was beneath the dignity of British royalty.

Trader Jon on a busy day.

"He was a nice sailor," says Trader of Prince Andrew. "Just a regular guy. He had a lot of moxie."

Unfortunately for Prince Andrew, the British tabloid press, which had dogged his every move, did not choose to think of him as a regular guy. The prince was royally roasted back in England for his visit to Trader's, though whether it was because of the strippers that inhabited the bar at night, or the prince's fearless journey into the jaws of the American Dream, was never made clear.

The uproar over the prince was a major topic of conversation in

Pensacola during a luncheon hosted by Mayor Vince Whibbs for local dignitaries and officers of the *Hermes*. Despite speculation that the prince would attend the function, he was noticeably absent, further galling the socialites who were appalled that the prince considered them of lesser importance than the ragtag band of strippers, sailors and aviators who called Trader Jon's home.

"He's a super guy and has a smashing sense of humor," one Hermes officer told the Pensacola *Journal,* referring to the prince. "He sees the ironic side of his position."

Officially, nothing was said about the prince during the luncheon, according to the newspaper, but the mayor, nonetheless, delivered a "touching" invocation and cheered "here, here" during toasts to the Queen of England. It was the least he could do.

Being a showpiece for one's country can be trying, noted the newspaper—especially for a young man with an entourage of bodyguards.

"Andrew is perfectly normal," says one of the prince's crew members. "And he has his father's eye for the ladies."

Trader remembers the day that Tennessee Williams, "smoking those little cigarettes of his," came in and sat in a barber chair in the back of the bar. Williams didn't say much, Trader recalls—just kept to himself. Just like legendary movie actor Henry Fonda, who wandered from picture to picture, never bothering to pull up a chair, staying in motion until he'd examined every item in the bar.

And, of course, Trader remembers the astronauts.

"They never came in as a group," he recalls. "Once they got outside that gate, they had separate times. It's a funny thing, the way they never grouped together. Alan Shepard, John Glenn—now there's a great guy—and Deke Slayton, there's another great guy. They never told anyone who they were. I was the only one who knew. We never spread their names around."

Thinking back to those hero-filled days of the late 1950s, Trader has no problem cataloging his memories: That's because in his heart, he, too, always will be an astronaut.

"They were in training here, helo training," he says. "Their studies were hard . . . and they were under 24-hour-a-day pressure. They never were relaxed with what they were doing, and the only way they could get relief was to get away and come to Trader's."

The astronauts, along with everyone else of substance who passed through Pensacola, came to Trader Jon's in search of their separate dreams.

Trader Jon, merchant of dreams. With his gritty smile and bulbous nose, he is one of the nicest, most compassionate men you could ever hope to meet.

"The place itself is a landmark for aviation people," says former Pensacola NAS commander Capt. D. B. Gilbert. "It's a way of saying hello to the old and goodbye to the new."

Although the Navy does not exactly sponsor Trader's as a naval

The Capsule John Glenn rode into space after training in Pensacola.

landmark, it does acknowledge—unofficially, of course—its debt to the bar. Capt. Gilbert, who in 1980 had been stationed in Pensacola for two years, says that while he doesn't go to Trader's often, he has been on several occasions.

Once he took his wife, but they made it a point to leave before the dancers took the stage.

"There's an attraction there to look back at the olden days of aviation," Gilbert says. "It's almost like a busman's holiday."

Trader gets high marks from the Navy.

"He's been known to help people out who were in trouble," says Gilbert. "Things like helping men get home in an emergency."

* * *

Whenever Trader's wife, Jackii, or either of their two adopted daughters—Dahn or Cheri—come into the bar it is always a cause for celebration. One day Jackii and Dahn came to the bar to talk over family business with Trader.

Since Trader works such odd hours—noon till three in the morning, seven days a week—such things often must be taken care of at the bar. In many ways, Jackii and Trader are alike. Either could pass, both in appearance and in actions, for the ideal grandparent—friendly, playful and never too busy to shoot the breeze with a customer with a bruised or broken heart.

Never anonymous when she visits the bar, most customers know Jackii by name and yell out to her, though always with great respect.

Trader Jon with wife, Jackii, and daughter, Dahn

If there is a newcomer in the bar, Trader sees that he does not long retain that status.

"Come on over here, Jackii," Trader says, extending his hand. "There's someone here I want you to meet."

And so it goes.

When Jackii and Dahn leave the bar, it is with the flourish of someone who walks away from a once-every-ten-years family reunion. Trader Jon's, unlike most of the other bars on the strip, has at its core a strong foundation built upon respect for family. That is why it is home away from home for tens of thousands of sailors, fly-boys, politicians, strippers, cowboys, runaways, movie actors, writers and sculptors.

Oh, yes, sculptors also are well represented at Trader's.

On the far wall, next to the stage, is a sculptured mural of nude

Bryan Proctor's mural.

male and female figures. Stretching from floor to ceiling, the mural is an impressive piece of artwork, so impressive, in fact, that Kodak once featured a photograph of the mural on the cover of its monthly magazine. The mural was done by Bryan Proctor, a well-known Pensacola architect who died in the late 1970s.

A former student of famed architect Frank Lloyd Wright, Proctor was well regarded by his colleagues. Trader places a value of $100,000 on the mural because "that's what he got for all his other work." A regular customer at Trader's, Proctor spent four months working on the mural. He did it as a gift for Trader.

"He just felt at home here and wanted to do something for

Trader," says Trader, speaking in the third person, as he sometimes does, drawing a distinction between himself and the legend. "Every few days he'd come in and sit around and work on it."

Once the work began, Trader built a wooden platform for Proctor so that he would be able to work more comfortably. Occasionally, he brought him a beer or two. "I never asked him what he was doing. He just kept pecking' away."

It says something about Trader Jon that a man could enter his bar, begin work on one of the walls without explanation—all without an inquiry from the bar owner.

Proctor never told anyone why he felt compelled to do the mural. Were visions of Michelangelo laboring beneath the ceiling of the Sistine Chapel dancing through his mind? No one knows. Proctor took the secret with him to his grave.

Out of respect for Proctor, Trader refrained from putting up a plaque identifying the mural as being the work of Proctor.

"A lot of people come and don't know who did it. But if they ask, I'll tell them."

Proctor is not the only artist who has found himself bewitched by the magic of Trader's bar. Jeff MacNelly, a two-time Pulitzer Prize-winning cartoonist, once drew a caricature of Trader while visiting the bar. Trader didn't put the drawing on the wall (it was too valuable for that) but he did use it in a newspaper advertisement.

Trader may have the sensibilities of an artist, but he has the

Trader Jon smoozes with afternoon regulars.

business acumen of a pragmatist.

"Trader's itself feels like a cartoon," MacNelly explained to the author before the cartoonist's death in 2000. "It's unique. There's no other place like it in the world."

MacNelly, an editorial cartoonist and creator of the comic strip "Shoe," first discovered Trader's while in Pensacola for a speaking engagement. "I thought it was great," he says of the bar. "Trader is one of the most generous people I've ever met. He's a classic."

Trader Jon sketch
drawn by Pulitzer
prize winner Jeff
MacNelly, America's
number 1 political
editorial artist
and creator of the
cartoon, Shoe.

$1,000 REWARD IF
YOU CATCH TRADER WITH MATCHING SOCKS!

This ad ran in Pensacola News-Journal (reprinted permission Jeff MacNelly)

3

KEEPING THE FAITH

January 1980

BEWARE BUFFALO, DO NOT ENTER—the hand-lettered sign atop the road-weary Chevy camper was not so much a warning as it was a protest. Next to the sign, beneath the tarpaper covering of the roof, was a star-studded likeness of Uncle Sam.

The American Dream: four years after the grandest, most expensive birthday celebration in American history. Somehow the faith had been kept. Just not the way everyone supposed.

Krystal Waterfalls piloted the unwieldy camper, named Abraxas after the Greek word for magic, off Interstate 10 into downtown Pensacola. On her way from Austin, Minnesota, to the South American country of Guatemala, Pensacola seemed a logical place to stop, especially since she was running low on money and needed a transfusion of cash to get them further down the road.

Krystal drives south on Palafox Street, her husband, Bush, on the

Bush and Krystal relaxing on their truck.

passenger side, and their dog Diablo, curled up between them. Krystal and Bush are on their way to Guatemala to join up with the Rainbow People, a nomadic commune of back-to-earth hippies. As part of their religious ceremony, members often smoke marijuana. They also work for nature conservation and the abolition of nuclear power plants. They are among the last spiritual remnants of the Woodstock generation.

Ever since Krystal's first husband disappeared with their son, she has wandered from city to city in search of her lost family, but with no luck. Now she only knows where they are not. The Rainbow People, dedicated to nature in its purest form, offer homes to both childless mothers and motherless children.

Although Pensacola is one of the oldest, most historical cities in Florida, Krystal's camper creaks right past the museums and tourist centers—straight to the tough, waterfront district of South Palafox. During the day, South Palafox looks like the main street of any number of small towns in Georgia or Alabama.

Sleepy, unhurried, with the buildings old and in disrepair, the street is a monument to another era in which people routinely stopped to talk to each other on the sidewalk.

Nighttime is different. Dark skies, dimly-lit sidewalks, and warm, salty breezes sliding in from the Gulf, all combine to create a Disneyworld atmosphere of adult fantasy. Music blares from the doorways of a half dozen topless go-go bars. Neon signs beckon tourists to see Pussy Galore, Foxy Lady, or Sweet Sue for the price of a beer, naked women, beautiful, suntanned, sanitized naked women. Naked, that is, but for a thread called a G-string.

Sex American-style.

Krystal pulls Abraxas over to the curb in front of the last bar on the strip. Only a block from the Gulf, Trader Jon's does not look like much in the daylight. With a wood exterior that has been weathered by sea air and constant rains, it resembles an abandoned warehouse. In fact, it once was a sail loft, a store that specialized in boating and sailing supplies. Two years earlier, when the streets were flooded by eighteen inches of unceasing rain, the author stood on top of a pickup truck and watched anxious rats swimming from one side of Palafox Street to the other.

Abraxas sputters to a stop.

"This it?" asks Bush, aroused from his nap.

"That's what the sign says."

"Uh, huh."

"You wait here," she says. "I'll go in and check it out."

Bush pulls his hat down over his eyes and curls up on the seat, his hand affectionately draped across Diablo's back. Bush is dog's best friend. They make quite a pair.

At the entrance, the massive wooden door, made of thick planking, is difficult to open, but she persists. Once inside, Krystal pauses at the entrance, allowing her eyes to adjust to the mid-afternoon darkness. Dressed in blue jeans, she has on hippie sandals and a colorful headband tied about her forehead, an acknowledgement of her Native American heritage.

The bar is deserted.

Martin Weissman, a.k.a. Trader Jon, stands behind the bar, alone, except for the author and the photographer of this book, who are seated at the bar chatting with Trader Jon.

Seeing Krystal in the doorway, Trader Jon pauses wiping the counter long enough to say, "Come on in," and then resumes work, with his eyes lowered..

Unsure of herself, Krystal smiles shyly, her hands stuffed into the

Trader Jon

front pockets of her jeans. Though she has heard stories about Trader Jon's from other dancers she met on the road, this is her first glimpse of the legendary bar.

Along the wall, pasted floor to ceiling, are hundreds of framed photographs. Pilots, astronauts, air force top-brass, movies stars—the list is endless. Some of the people in the photographs are famous. Some are not. Regardless of their fame, all are friends of Trader Jon. One could not ask for more than that.

"U.S. Navy Blue Angels: Defenders of Freedom," proclaims a banner at the rear of the bar. The Cradle of Naval Aviation, Trader Jon's is called—and with good reason.

From the ceiling, giant model airplanes hang, their wings tipped

Trader Jon begins his day talking care of his collection.

in mock flight as they circle about red and gold orbs glowing with the soft light of 25-watt bulbs. Near the door—and strung up almost out of sight—stare the hollowed-out eyes of a 160-year-old skeleton. Unearthed in Alabama, the skeleton of a 20-year-old girl was once owned by Dr. Robert Davis, a cousin of the former Confederate president Jefferson Davis. It's not easy to see the skeleton in the dim light, but, once spotted, it is practically impossible to ignore. Trader bought the bones for eighteen dollars. Perhaps for that reason, the fact that cash exchanged hands, the skull leers at passers-by, mildly threatening.

Krystal sits in one of the barbershop chairs at the bar. For thirty feet they wind into the dark, breaking for a walkway before circling back to the front—somehow, by then, magically transposed into ordinary barstools.

"What'll you have?" asks Trader Jon.

"A job."

Trader rests his arms on the swayback counter and looks the girl over. She wasn't knock-dead-gorgeous, but she wasn't ugly either.

"Ever danced before?" he asks.

"Plenty. I'm professional. You name it, I danced there."

Trader turns, motioning with his finger for her to follow. With a shuffling walk, he toddles over to the stage, his bony legs jutting bird-like from a pair of Bermuda shorts. In addition to the shorts, he has on a sweatshirt and a baseball cap.

Krystal walks behind him. She looks at his feet. He has on one blue sock and one red sock. His shoes are cutout army boots that have seen better days. Mismatched socks are Trader's trademark. He has offered a $1000 reward to anyone who can catch him with socks that match. Trader steps up to the two-foot-high stage. Rickety, with a well-worn linoleum floor, the stage is about sixty feet square. "Physical Fitness Clinic," reads a sign on the wall. In the corner is a giant speaker, part of an ancient Vox amplifier system. Trader reaches for a cassette to plug into the tape deck.

"No, I brought my own," Krystal says, reaching into her back pocket.

She hands the cassette to Trader.

Without glancing at the title, he puts it in the player and adjusts the sound. The music is loud, especially in a room empty of people. Krystal watches as Trader shuffles off the stage.

There is an eerie calm at mid-afternoon in Trader's, like sitting alone in a vast cavern. Even when the music is blaring there is a rainy-day moodiness about the place, a mood so powerful that it can slam an invisible door shut against the pounding of the music. It is easy to get lost in such a room.

Krystal begins to dance.

Dancing his fingers along the well-worn bar, Trader returns to the front. The music adds a slight bounce to his walk. Occasionally, he glances in Krystal's direction, but when he does, it is only for a brief

Spanish sailors exiting Trader Jon's, concerned their mothers might see this photograph-Photo by James L Dickerson

moment. It is not easy to jump out of a pickup truck that has been driven hard all day and then hop up onto a stage to dance for an empty house. Krystal did it with class. Twirling with the music, dipping in all the right places in the soundtrack, so that by the time she slipped off her shirt and twirled it with her index finger up over her head, she was in a seductive groove.

Trader busies himself at the bar, straightening the bottles already arranged in neat rows beneath the counter. His eyes dart back and forth to the stage, but never once does he stare. He knows it is tough for a woman to take off her clothes to audition for a job.

Trader likes to keep his distance as a way of giving her space.

45

Julie, the youngest dancer at the bar.

4

NIGHT MOVES

January 1980

By five o'clock, the bar has picked up a few office workers from downtown who have stopped by for a drink on their way home. The pace is a little faster now, the music a little louder. Cookie, Trader's only steady barmaid, is there now. Dressed in a black sweater and black jeans, she paces slowly among the empty tables, killing time. Since Trader tends the bar, and the tables won't be filled until seven o'clock, there's not much for her to do right now.

Cookie is working the pin ball machine when two men, the author and photographer of this book, arrive and sit at one of the tables. She glances over her shoulder at them, but the pinball machine is clattering and she is reluctant to leave a hot run. Finally, the last bell rings, and she sighs, her score not up to minimum standards.

Cookie saunters over to the table, pausing a moment before she speaks, seemingly to collect her thoughts.

"Can I get you anything?"

She smiles. Her gentle voice, like her movements, flows soft as a summer night.

"No . . . no thanks."

"Are you sure?" she asks in amazement.

"Thanks anyway," says the photographer, his eyes penetrating the darkest corner of the bar in search of available light.

"OK," she says, walking away.

Cookie talks to Trader Jon behind the bar. Then she returns. This time she pulls up a chair. "Trader says to let you have anything you want," she says, a newfound gleam in her eye. "You don't have to pay for it."

Again, the answer is no.

Cookie looks perplexed.

"You can have anything you want," a look of bewilderment on her face. "I've never seen him do that before."

Still the answer is no.

Cookie stares at the newcomers, shyly, the way a child stares from behind the safety of a closed window. When she speaks, there is a whiny twang to her voice; when she does not speak, she sits very still. Sometimes she sits so still she slips into a depression.

Cookie works at Trader's because the pay is good and because she has a son at home to support. Sometimes she gets up on stage, pulls her shirt off, and dances topless. She doesn't do that often, though, only when Trader asks her to as a special favor.

*   *   *

While sunlight still streams in past the opened door, Trader gets a bottle of window cleaner and makes his rounds. In one hand he holds the cleaner. In the other he holds a soft rag. Slowly, and with great care, he goes from picture to picture, scrubbing and polishing each pane of glass as though it was priceless.

Once every week he cleans the pictures. It is his way of keeping the faith. When he is dead and gone, he hopes that the pictures, along with the memory of Trader Jon's, will endure. But he doesn't figure that will be anytime soon.

"I'm just beginning," he grins. "This is the prime of the works. How could I retire?"

Customers file in at a steadier pace now.

They seem to be staying longer and drinking more.

Krystal is on stage. The music belongs to Willie Nelson and Waylon Jennings. Dancing at the edge of the stage, Krystal does her act. First, the jeans come off, then the shirt, then the tube top— finally down to her G-string.

Krystal is not an especially graceful dancer, but she is controlled, and her eyes send out sparks as she twirls, hands in air, her bare skin colored pink by the passion lights.

Outside the bar, her husband, Bush, and their dog, Diablo, are

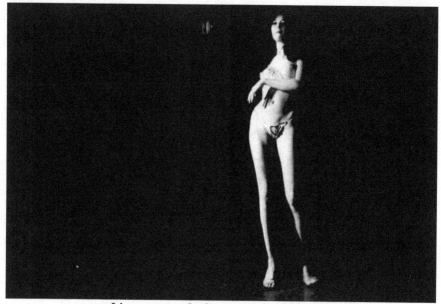

Lisa commands the stage when she dances.

sound asleep in the back of the truck. It has begun to rain, a slight mist that makes the slippery streets glisten. Backstage, in the dressing room, Rive and Julie slip out of their street clothes.

Up front, at the bar, sits Lisa. Wearing a flowery floor-length dress, she—with her high school cheerleader looks—is the very picture of sweetness and innocence. Her hair is dark, almost black, and it falls loosely to her shoulders. Cool on the outside, Lisa practically seethes on the inside, driven by forces she can neither identify nor explain. Something is pushing Lisa.

For years, Lisa, Trader and Tex have known each other. It is yet another example of the uniqueness of Trader Jon's: every artifact, every person, is connected in some way, all part of an endless circle of entangled relationships, each reeling outward like ripples across the surface of a pond.

While in school, Lisa and her younger sister became friends with Trader's daughters. Often, as a child, Lisa visited in Trader's home.

"I've known him since I was knee-high," says Lisa. "Trader has always been good to me in every sense of the word. I have a younger sister who is seventeen and she is the same age as Trader's youngest daughter, Cheri, and I used to take them to the recreation center in the summer. Trader is a hell of a nice guy. He'll never do you wrong unless you do him wrong first. If you do him wrong, he'll just write you off and not have anything else to do with you."

One day, Tex and Lisa went with Jackii and Cheri to buy a horse. The horse was meant to be a present for Cheri.

"They took me there to check it out," Tex explains. "So I threw a saddle on the horse and pulled him backwards and he fell down with me on top. I just picked the saddle up and walked back to the barn and left him lying there. You see, in the movies, when you're an extra in a western, you got to know how to trip a horse. Bang, you're dead! And you trip the horse and it falls down . . . and without knowing what I was doing, I give him a jerk and . . . bammmm! He went down. I caught his mouth just right, I guess, and he just backed up and went down."

Tex told Jackii and Cheri that the horse was not worth buying and

TJ making change for Cookie and at work in his office.

they left without explanation, the horse still down on the ground.

Sometimes you have to know when to walk away. And that was something Tex was good at—walking away.

Trader Jon's customers defy categorization. Sitting at the bar are the managing editor of the *Pensacola News-Journal*, an assortment of businessmen, and maybe a real estate agent or two. Out past the netting, beneath a sawed-off airplane wing, are a dozen or so naval cadets. Then, past them and closer to the stage, sits a mechanic, hunched over his drink, his hands still caked with grease.

Krystal finishes her act. There is a hard silence as she bends to pick up her things. Applause is not everything, she convinces herself. Naked, except for a G-string, Krystal stands on stage, waiting for Trader to say something. Already she has punched off the tape player. Silence hung over her like a dark cloud.

"Did I do OK?" she asks, a hint of insecurity in her voice.

"Bee-you-tee-full!" Trader purrs. "Put your clothes on and come back tonight. You got a job."

Krystal gathers up her clothes. She feels odd on stage with no audience. Thirty ice-cream tables and one hundred heart-shaped metal chairs sit clustered about her. Slowly, she dresses. There are no soft edges to lean on. The rule is simple: Stay balanced or fall flat on your face.

"Hey, put on some disco," shouts Trader.

With hard-driving disco again in the air, Krystal slips back into her jeans. She buttons up her shirt, and then she strolls past Trader on her way out.

"See ya' later," she says, smiling, then thinking *what a piece of cake!*

Meanwhile, in walk two cowboys wearing hand-tooled boots, brass belt buckles and J. C. Penny cowboy hats. They sit next to the wall, beneath Proctor's mural. Cookie takes their order. Beer. She smiles, but they don't smile back. These guys are leather tough. Just sitting at the table, their hands knotted up into fists. Dream busters.

Suddenly, the music was gone.

* * *

Backstage, Lisa, brushes her hair before going out on stage. She is next. Each girl does a ten minute set, working around the clock, seven until two in the morning.

Suddenly, Lisa hears her name announced.

Trader, using a microphone installed at the bar, introduces Lisa to an already impatient crowd. Lisa puts out her cigarette. Like most chain smokers, she is always extinguishing half-smoked cigarettes. She looks into the mirror one last time, checking out her hair.

Left behind in the dressing room, is Julie, who sits in silence, smoking. Rive is out mingling with the customers. When asked to sit down, she does so without speaking. Mostly she sits and smiles, trying not to offend.

On stage, Lisa is vibrant. The red beads of her costume reflect a thousand glimmers. She twirls, struts, every movement controlled and fluid. Lisa communicates: improvising a ballet of sexual fantasy. The music—a song by the Eagles called "Disco Dancer"—throbs with meaning for her.

Lisa has a natural ability for her work. Always cool, always in control. Light flashes from her dark eyes like pulsating strobes. She is a different person on stage: gone is the nervousness, the uncertainty about the future, the failures of the past . . . now Lisa is a star, the focus of every man's attention.

Never sullen, Lisa smiles constantly.

Take me, I'm yours, she seems to say with her body.

But from the grasps of each outstretched hand, she turns, never allowing anyone to touch her. For Lisa, the fantasy she performs on stage is her most direct link with reality. Hers is a topsy-turvy world. She is, for many men (and women) in the audience, the fulfillment of a hundred different sex-goddess fantasies, yet, for Lisa, it is no fantasy. It is her daily reality.

Oddly, no one in the audience feels cheated, you can see that on their faces. They clap—men and women alike—whistle, sing and follow her every move. A collective sigh washes back through the audience, followed by a moment of silence . . . that near waking point in a dream, when everything is so clear, yet fading so fast, so that only by slamming the brakes of consciousness is there any hope of retaining some small part of it.

Out in the audience, sitting at a table with friends, is a newcomer to Trader's. His eyes follow Lisa's movements matter-of-factly.

"You can't describe this to anyone," says Paul Cordieor, a U.S. Navy chief stationed in Pensacola. His father, Arthur Cordieor of Boston, also a navy chief, was stationed in Pensacola in the 1950s. "Dad told me to come here. He wouldn't tell me why. When I did, I knew why . . . This is the only place I have ever seen in the States where someone has had the nerve, or honesty, to say this is the way it should be. People come here to see the girls, sure, but mostly they come to see Trader."

Lisa slides from a chair she has pulled on stage, lowering herself to the floor, slowly, slithering with the slow smoothness of an exotic serpent. Then, sitting on the floor and moving in time with the music, she puts one hand on each foot and stretches out her arms, spreading her legs out into a giant V.

A hush falls over the crowd.

Expecting an as of yet unimagined obscene gesture to follow, the men in the audience pause at their drinks, bottles and glasses poised in mid-air. They are waiting for something major to happen. They have no idea what it is. Fantasies spiral out of control.

Lisa rises to her feet, smiling sweetly.

For her, it was a gymnastic trick, something learned in high school, nothing more. Aroused by the stares of the men, she prowls, catlike, along the edge of the stage, one last look into their eyes

Julie and Lisa

before she pulls the plug on their fantasies. With that gesture, she she lets them know that some things are never what they seem.

Trader makes frequent rounds, making sure everyone is happy. He pauses at one table to talk about Lisa.

"She's very good, very wonderful," Trader says. "They all are. I admire them. These girls want to work for a living, and they do. They work hard, and they're independent. I love them dearly. They never ask anybody for anything. I knew Lisa when she was a little kid. She always was a good girl, went to school, and never caused any trouble."

Lisa never caused anyone any trouble? Does that sound right? No, she never caused anyone any trouble, except maybe for herself.

"I was a rowdy little girl, a tomboy," Lisa says. "I still consider myself a tomboy. I ran away from home when I was thirteen . . . really, what I'd do was stay out to midnight, and my mom would call the law on me as a runaway. She didn't know what else to do. I was uncontrollable because I grew up so fast . . . ahead of my time. I was out on my own at sixteen, working at the Shrimp Box. I went to school and worked. That's just it, I always did what I wanted to do. It wasn't like regardless of who I hurt or because I was trying to hurt anybody. I was just trying to be myself, and live, you know."

After finishing her first set on stage, Lisa gathers her things and walks proudly, shoulders back, chin held high, to the dressing room. Never once does she try to cover herself as she walks past customers seated at the tables. Backstage, Lisa looks tired. Her breathing is heavy, the result of her acrobatics on stage.

"Great crowd tonight," she says. "In another few hours, it'll really be something."

* * *

Wearing only a G-string, Lisa carefully hangs her costume on a row of water pipes that serve as the room's only closet. Half-filled

Lisa enjoying a quiet moment.

with a giant, walk-in refrigerator used to cool beer, the dressing room is as bare and stark as a prison cell.

One wall is brick and is painted pink. Another wall, made of rough cypress, is unpainted. In a corner are rolls of tarpaper roofing material and a rickety old gas heater that moans and groans as if every blast of heat will be its last.

On one wall have been tacked two waist-high mirrors. They are above a table that serves as a vanity for the dancers. The table is covered with a red-checked tablecloth and littered with lotions, mineral oils, cosmetics, body powders, boxes of glitter and hair spray. Near the table is an enormous stuffed dog, about three feet tall, standing ready to be hugged at a moment's notice when needed.

At regular intervals, the refrigerator, which resembles a great, black tomb, kicks on with a jarring roar. The motor is so loud that only Trader's amplified voice can be heard above the din. Attached to the wall, up above the mirror, is a handwritten sign: "No showing your Kooter or any flashing—fired immediately, Trader Jon."

Rive sits on one side of Lisa, Julie on the other. Krystal, by now, has ventured out to talk with the customers. In the dressing   Lisa lights a cigarette, one of many she will smoke that night. Then she slips off her G-string. Now she is completely nude. She sits in one of the battered kitchen chairs at the dressing table. Stuffing hangs from the chair and it is so shaky it looks as if it could fall apart at any moment and dump her to the floor.

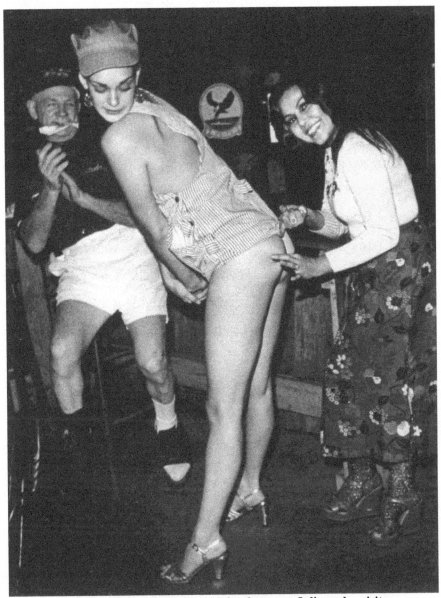

Trader enjoying the interaction between Julie and a visitor.

At ease with her nudity—and not in the least embarrassed—Lisa later will stand before the mirror and leisurely groom her hair with a brush she has picked up from the table, oblivious to the writer and photographer in the room. For the moment, she is dead tired. Content to sit and smoke.

In the dressing room, the talk is about about men.

"Some guy walked up to me last night, and he said, 'I'm gonna get you,' and that's as point-blank as you can get," Lisa says.

She sits with both feet on the floor, hardly aware of the attention she has attracted from others in the room. Milky white, Lisa has no suntan markers. Her skin is flawless, unmarked. Her legs, unlike the legs of many veteran strippers, have not a single bruise or blemish.

"I just smiled at him," Lisa continues, laughing. "Like, take your best shot, buddy!"

Lisa is a firm believer in democracy.

The other girls smile, for they know the routine.

"You have to keep them happy," says Lisa. "They're your people. You have to make them understand, hey, if I like you, I like you. You take a girl who has a fantastic body and gets up there to dance and doesn't smile, she isn't going to get anything from the audience. But you take me, skinny me, I get up there and smile every now and then, and they go crazy."

There is only one telephone in Trader's, a pay phone. Nestled away between the pin ball machines, it is barely noticeable, except

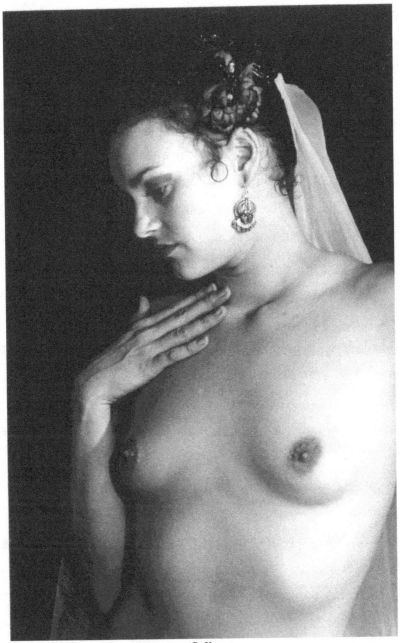

Julie

when it rings. This time it is for Lisa. She is ready to go on stage, but she tosses a wrap over her costume and takes the call. It is from her husband. Lisa and Ronnie met when she was fifteen.

"We dated two or three times, and that was it," she says. "Then I came back after being gone for a long time and I ran into him again and we just hit it off. I threw away my birth control pills. Ronnie didn't know anything about it. I didn't tell him. I made up my mind I wanted one 'cause I love kids so much. I used to baby-sit. I had one that was six, one that was seven, one that was eight months and one that was two years old, and I used to keep them all day, from eight in the morning until five. The baby grew up calling me mama, and ever since then I've wanted a baby so bad."

Lisa's baby is now seven months of age, pretty like her mother. Named Liz, she seems exceptionally bright. Always touching, reaching out, exploring her surroundings, she seems driven by the same sense of curiosity that has made Lisa such an uninhibited free spirit. If she is not held when she wants to be picked up, she cries out with an urgent, deep-throated wail that demands immediate obedience.

Lisa tries to be firm with Liz in a cranky, but not mean, sort of way, but in the end she always relents and lets her have what she wants. The reason why is not hard to understand.

"I can only have one more, so I'm going to cherish this one to the end," says Lisa. "I had a Cesarean, and I had a really rough time and

Lisa dressing to go home.

she almost died. So they're only going to let me have one more."

Lisa grimaces when she thinks about it.

"I had these red lumps on my stomach where they were giving me miracle drugs to keep me alive. At $150 a shot, four times a day in the stomach."

Like many pregnant women, Lisa decided to work until she was six months into her pregnancy. Surprisingly, she got away with it.

"Oh, I had a little tummy there, but that was it," she says with a glint in her eye. Within four weeks after her delivery, she was back at work, strictly against the orders of her doctor, bumping, grinding, doing The Act.

Lisa

5

BEWARE OF BUFFALO RIDERS

January 1980

Julie puts the final touches on her hair. She goes on stage next.

"Men will be men," she says. "I enjoy a man's company. I feel no hostility unless I get a lot of b.s. from them. The ones I know are straightforward and truthful with me. I love them. But the ones who try to feed you a line of baloney, I get tired of them. I could just as soon do without them."

Tall—about five-feet-eleven-inches—and well proportioned, Julie is the youngest of Trader's dancers. Slender, with soft brown eyes that vacillate between moods of gentleness and outrage, Julie has long arms and legs that are deceptively strong.

When Julie dances, her calf muscles knot up into tight balls and the strength of her arms is clearly indicated by her slightly rounded biceps, yet her muscles are those of a professional athlete, such as a long distance swimmer, and not those of a mannish woman. Wearing a colorful harem outfit, Julie leaves the dressing room and heads for the stage. There is a wild stare in her eyes. On stage, she seems dazzled by the lights.

Left alone in the dressing room, Lisa and Rive open a box of fried chicken someone has left for them. Sometimes they eat beef stew, other times hamburgers, whatever they can get people to bring them.

Rive is the quietest of Trader's dancers and she has little to say to anyone. Mostly she watches the others. There is a very gentle quality about her. A stranger meeting her for the first time on the street would never guess that she is a dancer, since she looks more like a secretary or someone's mother or sister.

Backstage talk takes many strange twists and turns. From where to purchase quality ground beef to the cheapest place to fill up their cars. Eventually the conversation turns to more serious matters, such as turning tricks.

Julie says she has been offered solicitations more often than she can count. "I've always turned them down," she explains. "I don't have to turn tricks. Maybe I'm stupid. Maybe I'd be rich by now. If I wanted to turn tricks, I wouldn't be working in a place like this. I'd be uptown somewhere, making that money. I guess you could say I have thought about it, but not for long. It comes into my head and goes out."

Dancer doing her routine for admirers.

Lisa startles everyone by saying that she has turned a trick. Necks snap. Eyes bulge. Lisa? *Our* Lisa? If they looked closer they would see a devilish smile breaking at the corners of her mouth. They stare, waiting for an explanation . . .

"Not a real trick, silly," she laughs. "There was this guy who liked to be made a fool out of. He paid me two hundred dollars and he came to my house and he put on a dress and he put on makeup. His name was Bob and I called him Barbara. That's what he wanted me to call him. He liked for me to tell him to do things like, 'Clean that chair,' and use vulgar words. I made him give me a bath. I made him cook. I made him clean the whole house. I made him get down on his knees and lick my shoes. It was what he wanted, you know. I led him around the house with a belt, shit like that. And I got paid two hundred dollars for doing that, and I consider that a trick. Shit man, two hundred dollars to have somebody clean my house!"

The other dancers smile, eyes glowing.

A true fantasy of their secret sisterhood.

* * *

On stage, Julie is a crowd-pleaser. Long stems, spontaneous, she projects a sensual wildness on stage. Spinning like a top, she reaches upward, her costume swirling out like a fisherman's net. Faster, faster—until, stepping too close to the edge of the stage, her high-heel shoe slips off, tossing her to the floor. Unaffected, she rises to her feet with the help of a customer. More swirls, more dips

Julie walking offstage.

and lunges.

Between acts, Trader often takes to the stage to keep the momentum going. It is his finest hour.

"I'm offering a $100 prize to the person who can jump the highest on a pogo stick," he announces, holding the microphone close to his lips. With his other hand he guides the cord, the way masters-of-ceremony do in the glitzy Las Vegas nightclubs.

Alas, there is not a single pogo stick in the audience.

Undeterred, he announces a pushup contest.

First prize is a bottle of champagne. Sounds easy enough. The stage fills with muscular young seamen eager to get something for nothing.

But there is a catch. Each contestant must do his pushups with one of the dancers or barmaids clinging to his back. The men grunt and groan, but no one backs off the stage. With the girls lying full-length across their backs, the men pump themselves up and down. Veins pop out on their arms like cords of twice-knotted rope.

Always, there is a winner in Trader's club.

Trader is a natural-born showman. If he had not gone into the bar business, he says he could have been a salesman. Certainly he has a unique talent for dealing with people. Everyone knows Trader; and anyone who has ever met Trader, cares about him.

During the ominous final days of President John Kennedy's administration, the president went to Cocoa Beach, Florida, to attend

Trader Jon MC's a push-up contest.

a party for the astronauts. Of course, Trader—flown there by the astronauts—was there to greet the president.

"He was glad to meet me, and I was glad to meet him," Trader recalls.

To the affair, Trader wore mismatched socks, shorts and a baseball cap.

"Kennedy was just a great guy. Very, very simple, and he was radiant with . . . just radiant. You could tell he had something very, very nice. He was just an ordinary guy with a lot of know-how and respect. He met you at your own level. He didn't put himself above you. He was very, very quick."

Backstage, Julie flops down into a chair. Her face is flushed from the exertion. Sweat drips down her chest to her belly. She turns on an electric hair dryer. Her hair, deep black and coarse, is soaked. After she dries her hair, she sits, legs crossed, and brushes it over and over again.

When Julie speaks, her words come out fast, like the rat-tat-tat of a machine gun. She takes no prisoners.

* * *

Lisa glides from one table to another, arms outstretched. If she had not been a stripper, she would have made a perfect Southern hostess. She has a way of making small talk seem like large talk. A flattering word here, a playful poke there, so that when she leaves a table after only spending a moment or two, those seated at the table

Dancer slips into a groove.

are left smiling, hoping for more of the same before the night ends.

Always, she stays away from the table where the Buffalo Riders are seated. They are cold, forbidding—untouchable in their firm, hard-eyed way, staring . . . dream-busters atop a great electronic buffalo, lights flashing, imaginary hoofs chipping off sparks like Fourth of July fireworks. In and out of the lights they toss, snarling and gritting their teeth. Beware of the electronic buffalo riders, the dancers whisper among themselves—pass the word, if you value what's left of your life. These men do not like women. Beware!

While the music still plays, Lisa sits beside a friend who has just come into the bar. Soon she is sitting on his lap, her arm draped across his shoulder, buddy-buddy-style. They talk to each other in soft, sleepy voices.

"I like to meet people," says Lisa. "I like to get to know them. I like to know what they're thinking, what they're feeling. I like to go out with them. I just like, you know, to feel free. You're not going to be here forever."

Late at night, Tex waxes into melancholy. Sitting with a group of his old buddies, he keeps an eye on whoever is dancing. Tex, says, "Girls are nice, no matter whether you lived a hundred years ago or today, beauty is in the eye of the beholder. If a guy looks on the bright side of life, he's gonna realize they're nice. You know, even me, at my age, I'm still as romantically inclined toward the womenfolk as when I was young."

Julie arranging her costumes on back patio

* * *

Outside the dressing room, the tempo of the music has changed. So has the dancer. At Trader's request, Cookie has taken the stage. The music is slow, just the type of music Cookie grooves on. Her movements are graceful, suspended in slow motion.

After the first song, Cookie takes off her sweater. The crowd is noisy, excited. She fulfills a fantasy many men have of seeing a perfect stranger—the woman on the street—disrobe in public. It's an old ploy, but it works every time.

At the end of the second song, Cookie stops dancing. She picks up her sweater from the floor and goes backstage. She sits in one of the rickety chairs, the sweater wadded in her lap. She looks at herself in the mirror and sighs.

"I dance every once in a while," she explains. "Trader talks me into it. Sometimes I don't mind as much as other times. Like tonight. I really didn't want to, but I didn't mind. Sometimes I just plain don't feel like it. I tell Trader no, I don't want to, and he won't make me. Tonight I'd been drinking a little bit, so I really didn't mind too much."

Over the loudspeaker, Rive hears Trader introduce her act. Always she is an exotic princess from a South Sea island.

Rive grimaces each time she hears the spiel, but she smiles at the same time. Deep down inside she is pleased that he makes a big fuss over her. Rive was slow to learn the ropes of the business; but now

Rive does her makeup as Lisa eats fried chicken in the dressing room.

she is a pro, dedicated to each bump and grind.

On stage Rive's shyness is evident only in her eyes. Her movements are bold, confident. Bending at the knees, down into a squat, she snaps her arms with sudden, crisp movements. Rarely does she smile, except when her eyes wander and she makes eye contact with someone in the audience she recognizes. Then, turning to the side, she tries to hide her smile, dancing with her back to the audience.

As Rive dances, the door to the dressing room creaks open.

"Lisa!" squeals a sailor in a high voice. He sticks his head inside the door, his shiny smooth face red with rum.

"Just a minute! Don't come into the dressing room."

Lisa comes to her feet. She, along with the other dancers,

Lisa says fried chicken is better when enjoyed naked.

hurriedly covers herself.

Gently, Lisa nudges the sailor away from the door. He leaves without complaint, pleased he was permitted to cross the sacred threshold, even for the briefest of moments. Lisa is good with men. Always at ease, always in control. That's the way she likes it.

"I grew up with all guys," Lisa says. "I had a few girlfriends, but most of them I didn't get along with because they were jealous of me or I was jealous of them. I feel a lot more comfortable with men, you'd better believe it, because I can talk to them. I think they understand me, and most women don't. A lot of women are like this—they think if a girl is pretty or if she dances or something like that, they think she's trying to take their boyfriend or husband away.

I don't know why that is, but every time I get a girlfriend, and . . . see, like it's me and her and a date and her boyfriend or husband, they always think I'm trying to take their boyfriend away from them, and maybe even I don't talk to them, I just try to be nice. I don't know what it is. I don't understand it. But I can't live with girls, that's one thing I cannot do. We end up in a big fight, and that's why I don't have a girl roommate."

Rive's shoes pop like wooden blocks across the concrete floor of the dressing room. It is midnight, and the crowd outside, fortified by two-dollar drinks, is as raunchy and unpredictable as a wild-west rodeo on steroids.

"It's wild hysteria out there," Rive says, her eyes wide with excitement.

Slowly, the door opens, silently, as though it is being nudged by the wind. In the dark beyond the door is a face. It is the face of a man with a full beard.

"May I come in?"

"Yeah, just shut the door behind you," Krystal says. She looks up for only a moment. She is putting on her makeup. Serious business.

Uncertain of what to do, the man slips into the room. He's dressed in worn jeans, a flannel shirt and a floppy hat. The man yawns, his still-sleepy eyes cast downward.

"This is him," Krystal says, introducing her husband, Bush, to the others in the room. Quietly, Bush stands out of the way, over against

Lisa is the most athletic of the group.

the wall. He knows he is out of his league.

Suddenly, in walk some of the barmaids—a Chinese woman who only works sporadically at Trader's. She had decided to dance, but cannot find the music she knows.

"Where is that tape?" she asks, her voice chattering in an unknown Asian dialect.

"It's up on the stage, the red one," Lisa says. "The one you danced to last night. The red tape."

"I dunno what one," she says.

"OK, let me put something on" Lisa says.

Still wearing only a G-string, she throws on a transparent wrap to go out into the bar. Looking back over her shoulder at a visitor she explains, "I don't want to be attacked or anything."

She looks at herself in the mirror.

"Boy, lot of good this does."

"It makes you legal," Krystal says. "Makes you legal."

"I ain't never been legal in my life," Lisa laughs.

"Anybody got any cigarettes?" asks Krystal. "Lisa, you got any cigarettes back here?"

"No, not here."

Rive says, "I've got some, if you smoke menthol."

"Yeah, I'll take anything right now. I just need a cigarette."

Krystal takes a cigarette from Rive.

"Thank you," she says. Then she screws up her face in disgust. "Filters with fiberglass! Ugh!"

Later, after finishing the menthol cigarette, Krystal reaches over and takes a pack from Bush's shirt pocket.

Bush says, "You're not gonna steal all my cigarettes now, are you?"

"I wasn't intending on stealin' all your cigarettes," says Krystal.

"Don't you know that when you're with a woman, all you have belongs to her?" says Lisa. "You haven't figured that out yet?"

Krystal says, "Sweetheart, what's yours is mine, and what's mine is mine."

"That's right," Lisa says.

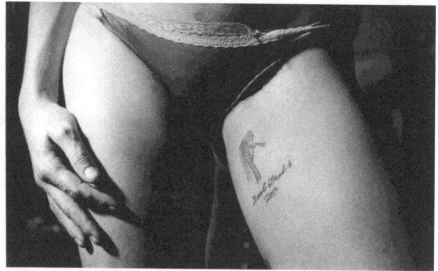

Krystal's message to the world: Don't tread on me.

Bush shakes his head. He's outnumbered and he knows it.

Soon Krystal is on stage again. This time Bush takes a table near the stage. Krystal seldom glances his way. Once, with her breasts bare, she leans off stage, above a table where six sailors are seated. When one of the men lunges forward, she grabs his head and presses his face to her skin, but it is only against the bony part of her chest between her breasts. He is not touching her breasts.

Bush looks away. Though he doesn't comment, it is obvious he does not like what he has just seen. Still, it is unlikely he would complain. That would violate the terms of their relationship. When they married, their agreement was that the person who could make the most money would work; the other partner would stay at home and keep house.

Trader answering the only telephone in the bar.

"I'm into lost knowledge," explains Bush, his speech slow and ponderous. "Much of what man has learned has been forgotten. Like the things learned by the Indians. By looking for lost knowledge, I'm trying to expand my head space. I've already found some knowledge. That's the meaning of my life."

When her song ends, Krystal gathers up her clothes and sits at the table with Bush, dressing as she talks to the author who has joined them. "There are lots of farms that belong to the Rainbow People, and I'm a member," she explains. "At the Woodstock gathering we discovered we could put a couple thousand people together and have a good time and learn a bunch of stuff and nobody get in trouble."

85

Trader Jon with his new logo.   Photo by James L. Dickerson

She pauses, slipping into her jeans.

"OK, so we're going for it," she says, proving that she can dress and talk at the same time. "Every year, up in the mountains, we have what's called the Rainbow Family healing gathering. What we are is a highly-knit, loosely-organized society that wants to bring back the Native American way of life. When people from the cities hear about us, they come to our gatherings and we start de-programming what television has done to them."

Bush nods knowingly to every point at Krystal makes.

"What is important to me is the preservation of our forests— natural lands and wildlife," Krystal continues as she buttons her shirt. "I've been to almost every rally against nuclear power there has been. I've helped set up three different reserves for wildlife. We try to show how to live in harmony with nature. I hope to be in Guatemala for the major part of this winter."

Krystal and Bush see themselves as messengers.

Trader Jon's is little more than a postmark along their journey.

* * *

After her last act, Lisa will change into her jeans, and along with Julie, go to one of the several "bottle clubs" in Pensacola. Bottle clubs are disco palaces where, because it is after hours, you have to take your own liquor. There she'll stay, dancing with everyone in the club, her eyes bright with expectation, until daylight. Then it's back to Terry and Liz, and the start of another day.

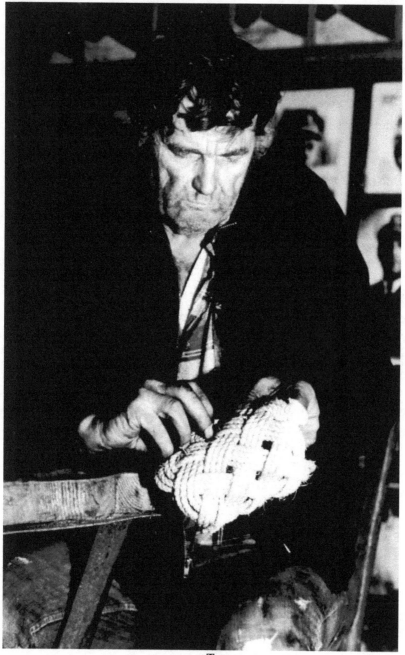

Tex

6

THE WILDERNESS MAN

Trader smiles back at Krystal as she leaves. Then, then seeing a tall, lanky man in the doorway, he says, "Come on in, Tex." Richard "Tex" Sullivan pauses, holding the door open for Krystal. Then he sits at the bar where he can talk to Trader.

Friends since the 1950s, they have covered a lot of ground together. Tex is twelve years Trader's junior, but, with his rugged, sea-burned face, he actually looks much older. He first started coming to Trader's in the 1950s, when he was a sailor. Then he came to drink and to watch the women.

But time is a burden to men like Tex. Now when Tex stops by Trader's it's more in search of conversation than anything else. He hardly ever orders a drink, and Trader hardly ever offers free drinks, even to his good friends.

"Tell me again about John Wayne," Trader says, tossing a wink in the direction of a writer sitting at the bar. "You were a great friend of Wayne's . . . go on, tell me about him."

Tex, his speech slow and drawn out, remembers the day Wayne first came into Trader's. Wayne was in Pensacola to make a movie called the *Wings of Eagles*.

"I was working on that wheel," Tex says. His voice is raspy, and the words roll out rough and gritty, like shoe leather on gravel. "When, you know, he comes in the door, he had on a pair of Levis and a pair of sneakers. I heard everybody holler HURRAH, and I looked around, not sure what to expect."

"Who in hell is he?" I asked.

"He saw me working on that wheel, and he come up."

"Hey, I like that," he said.

"I said, you look familiar to me."

"Well, I should. I'm John Wayne."

From that point on, Tex and Wayne were friends.

When Wayne left Pensacola, he took with him the ship's wheel Tex had worked on. Later, it was mounted on Wayne's yacht *The Wild Goose*.

Tex is particular about his memories. He works them the way he would a complicated sailor's knot. He remembers John Wayne as being very quiet and unassuming.

"He was cool," Tex says. "He never got frantic. He never got excited about nothing. If somebody made a wrong statement, he just passed it off as part of the script. He was a remarkable human being."

Tex, who knows the secrets of four hundred different knots—skills learned from more than thirty years at sea—has a knack for meeting up with movie stars. During the late 1950s and early 1960s, after John Wayne had befriended him at Trader's, Tex worked as a Hollywood stunt man and extra at Review Studios, a subsidiary of Universal Studios. Review Studios specialized in westerns made-for-television, shows like "Sugarfoot" and "The Virginian."

"I starved to death," says Tex. "There was a lot of work, but no money. A guy kept telling me, hang around and you'll get your break . . . I said, yeah, big break."

Nonetheless, Tex did get to meet many of his favorite movie stars. That was worth something. A memory or two, if nothing else.

"Gary Cooper was my main man," says Tex. "When he made *High Noon*, that's when I identified with him because, secretly, that was what I wanted to be—the sheriff of a western town."

Tex got a chance to meet his hero in 1958, during the filming of *The Hanging Tree*. Tex had a small part in the western—"So small, you wouldn't know it unless it was pointed out to you"—which stared, in addition to Cooper, George C. Scott, Karl Malden and Maria Schell. An adaptation of Dorothy Johnson's short story, the movie had Cooper playing a Montana doctor, and Karl Malden, a lecherous gold miner who lusted after Maria Schell.

The Hanging Tree was one of Cooper's last movies. Although he was dying of lung cancer at that time and had less than three years to live, there were no outward signs of his fatal illness. Friends remarked that they had never seen him happier.

For the first time in several years, Cooper was pleased, not only with his movies, but with his personal life. After a long separation from his wife, Sandra Shaw, they had reconciled and started anew. On the day they wrapped production on *The Hanging Tree*, the Coopers held a party for the cast. Tex was among those invited.

At the party, Tex struck up a conversation with Sandra. He told her about his sailing days, and about his unique talents with rope.

"I told her I could make dancing costumes," Tex says. "And she said she wanted to see. So I ended up making her one of parachute cord. I made the halter and leggings like you've seen these African chiefs wear. You know, the kind they put chicken feathers in."

Sandra was grateful for the costume, but she did not offer to model it for Tex.

"No, she wouldn't do that," he says, horrified that a writer would even ask such a thing. "She wanted it because it was something she couldn't run around to the store and buy."

Years later, Tex was driving his 1966 Pontiac station wagon to Las Vegas to meet his brother, when fate grabbed him where it hurts. Although he didn't yet know it, he was halfway to Australia and a mysterious paradise known as Dunk Island.

"I'm driving my car down Las Vegas Boulevard and here stands this funny little man in a checkered suit," explains Tex. "He's hitchhiking, you know, and I was driving along in the curb lane and stopped for a red light and he stuck his head in the car."

"Hey, they've cleaned me out down there," said the man in the checkered suit. "How about giving me a ride to the hacienda?'

Continues Tex: "I took him up to the hacienda and we got to talking. He was a chiropractor. He went on about a boat he owned and I thought he was just shooting the breeze. But he gave me his card. He says, 'I've got a schooner in Chicago and I want to go to Australia and I need somebody to go along who knows sailboats and the sea.'

"I said, 'Hey, that's me!'

"When I got home—I lived in Detroit then—I called, and sure enough he was there, and he invited me down and I seen the boat. So I went aboard. It was a good-looking boat, a gaff-rigged schooner. Oh, it must have been a hundred years old.

"So we went up the St. Lawrence Seaway, down around Panama, Tahiti . . . and then we put in at Botany Bay [discovered by Captain Cook in the 1700s]. From Botany Bay, we took Cook's exact course all the way up to Dunk Island.

"We tied the schooner on the mainland and went over to Dunk Island and we spend about fourteen months there, poking around and all that. It's a fantastic place, and I found out the Australians themselves are partial to Dunk Island. But they don't publicize it because they don't want the world invading their summer recreation area."

With the money he earned on the cruise with the chiropractor, Tex returned to Pensacola and bought a camper. The last he heard, the chiropractor was still walking the beaches of Dunk Island, searching for his lost dreams.

Obsessed with his memories of Dunk Island, Tex has spent every waking hour since the trip reliving the adventure. With him, he carries a dog-eared journal, a testament to his high-seas adventure. Reads the journal:

> **There are plenty of alligators here. Several times they were seen swimming across the lagoon. They are fierce. Once a wild buffalo started swimming across and was spotted by a huge, ugly-looking alligator. The alligator nailed it by his head and drowned it. The next morning, being Sunday, I got in my boat and drifted along the shore. The sea was like a sheet of glass, the heat of the sun was intense, with the glare from the sea almost blinding me. I went ashore in the afternoon with my rifle to shoot some ducks and geese. All the grass and reeds were burnt from the heat of the sun. The swamps were flat, many miles long, and there were only small patches of water. In the cool of the evening, the banana birds commenced their singing. It was a**

sign of a coming nor'easter, banking clouds, and terrific squalls, with tremendous rain, were evident.

A few days after the rain I took my boat out again and drifted farther down the shoreline. I landed in a nice sandy beach on the other side of the island where the beautiful foliage ran right up to the water's edge.

Tex walked through the forest, which resembled a jungle more so than any forest he had ever seen in mainland U.S.A. Red mangroves were everywhere. He was shocked to see flying foxes by the thousands hanging upside from the tree limbs. They are called flying foxes, but actually they are fruit bats that resemble fruit. Perhaps for that reason they prefer mangroves as their favorite hanging places.

I found green turtles in great numbers. The turtles reach a length of five feet. They are good in soup, and the flesh is like steak. During breeding season they deposit their eggs at night in the sand. With their powerful flippers, they dig briskly. They lay their eggs, shovel the sand over them, and go back into the sea.

* * *

Nearly a quarter century ago, Tex made one of those decisions that don't come too often in a man's life. He decided to get married. The woman he chose worked at Trader's as a dancer. Her name was Faye. No last name. No middle name. Just Faye. The marriage

A much younger Tex

lasted only about three months, and Tex never again succumbed to the temptation to marry. Thinking about it, though, still makes him angry. It seems that his wife, his "one and only" true love, was already married to someone else at the time she married Tex. He took news of the betrayal hard. Who knew that a dancer would ever be less than honest about her past?

No one in the bar told him about Faye's other life.

"I wasn't the one who found out about it," Tex says. "The Navy did. She told me not to make her out an allotment, and I thought there was something funny about that, and I knew that I couldn't run her down because I didn't have the money to hire somebody to do that. So I went to the dispersing office and told them I had reason to believe that my wife was married to someone else. That involved government funds, so naturally they were gonna run her down. They did, and they found out she was married to this other guy, drawing his allotment and mine."

Trapped by his memories, Tex does more watching these days than doing. He watches the customers sliding in and out of the barber chairs. Many of them during the afternoon hours are women. Some are very young, and come dressed in jeans. They don't wear bras and some of them talk very tough. The F-word is their sharpest weapon and they sometimes fill the air with it.

When they get angry and stab the air with their finger, venting because someone has asked to sit with them, their breasts dance beneath their T-shirts, a momentary distraction and nothing more.

"Yeah, well, the old people who came in when I came are still coming in—they haven't changed at all," says Tex. "But the young people, they're just not the same. I hate to pass an opinion on the younger generation, it's not my thing, but I find a number of things wrong with the young people of today. They're too influenced by what somebody else says, for one thing, and that's what makes them go wrong.

"If they would just use their own brains and to hell with what Joe Blow over there says, they'd be all right. There's nothing wrong with today's young people, except that there's too much pressure being put on them. I had the same pressure when I was their age, and nothing has changed in that respect. You know, the American system is never going to change. There is no way to beat it . . . I FOUGHT FOR THAT FLAG . . . still, being in America is better than being over in Iran or someplace."

Tex looks more like a cowboy than most cowboys. More like a seaman than most sailors. He looks tough, mean as a junk-yard dog, yet appearances can be deceiving. Although his jaw, set hard and square as a pine box, looks like it could chew through a two-by-four in one bite, it is used for talking, not fighting.

His long, muscular arms, made tough by years of pulling and tugging against ship cables, are used mostly for tying knots and holding doors open for young ladies who avoid eye contact with him as they walk past, a whiff of their perfume their only thanks.

"I literally let people walk all over me," he confesses. "I do it because I don't want to hurt anybody. So I'll let the guy get away with it because long as he doesn't hit me with a club, I'll be OK . . . I don't give a damn what a guy says to me. He don't hurt me. When you go to sea and you hear that wind blowing through the riggings, that's what it reminds me of, a strong wind blowing through the riggings. Play it cool, I say, and it'll run its course. If a guy comes in here and bad-mouths me, I sit here and pretty soon he's gonna get tired and go away."

Tex pauses, perhaps lost in a flashback of a distant memory; then he continues, "Unless he makes a move towards me, and that's when he's hurt."

*   *   *

As the day wears on, customers filter into Trader Jon's.

At that time of the day they are after a drink, not a peek at the girls, so they do not stay for long. Sitting in a corner, away from the traffic of the door, Tex seems uneasy in the tiny metal chair upon which he has chosen to perch.

Wearily he clutches his manuscript. He has dreams of becoming a world famous author. An explorer of the likes of Vasco Nunez de Balboa, who crossed Panama in 1513 to reach the Pacific Ocean. He carries his tattered manuscript with him the way some people carry Social Security cards, for identification.

Tex's teeth have long since departed and he appears in bad health, but he insists he has never felt better in his life. "My sailing days are over," Tex says sadly. "I spent, all-told, at least fifteen years at sea, if you add it all up. I don't like to go back to sea now, mainly because of the new people sailing. I mean, they shove me in the corner and say I don't know what I'm talking about . . . sit down and shut up, they say . . . I try to tell them about the old sailing days, but they don't want to hear that. They've got their own conception of it and they're not open to modifying their opinions."

During a lull in the conversation, Tex looks about the room, looking for something to talk about. A twinkle suddenly appears in his eyes. "See that pirogue," he says, pointing to an ancient canoe hung from the ceiling. "Back when the Indian Chief Geronimo was held prisoner out on the island, they used to have to take him back and forth to the mainland by boat. They had about 10 of these pirogues, and this one you see here was one of the original boats they used to transport Geronimo."

The island that Tex refers to is Fort Pickens, located across the bay from Pensacola. Geronimo and about a dozen other Native American warriors were held as prisoners of war at the fort for nearly two years before being relocated first to Alabama and then finally to Oklahoma Territory.

Tex moves over beneath the canoe and raps his knuckles against the bow. "See, it's solid through and through."

That conversation finished, Tex returns to his chair and sputters to a stop like a wind-up toy.

Tex has more past than future, and that's what keeps him going, always looking back to better days, better times. If you follow his footprints, they always lead back to Trader's.

"It isn't the dancers that bring me back," Tex says. "It's the nostalgia. The memories . . . When I was in the Navy, I frequented here all the time. Trader and I were such good friends and I knew everybody here. I just kept coming back, time and time again. I mean, actually, the town has done nothing for me, and I've done nothing for the town, but I come back to Trader's because I want to recapture the past."

* * *

There is sadness in Tex's eyes these days.

There is something about the way he carries himself that betrays his preoccupation with the past.

Tex thinks often of Trader.

He says, "It just does something for me to see Trader still on his feet. It makes me more secure knowing that an old friend of mine is still around. It gives me hope to carry on."

Tex doesn't like to think about what will happen when Trader dies, yet it's always lurking in the back of his mind. Death—it pulls at his memory, creating emotional tension.

"I'm kinda' partial to Trader. He's given me encouragement

when I was depressed, a word of advice. Nobody is so smart he can't take advice from somebody else. I don't know whether this is found in a quote or not, but you show me a man who's so big he can't take advice from somebody else . . ."

His voice trails off, ringing hollow with sadness.

Tex's head lowers, as if in prayer; then, moments later, he looks up and springs to life, his spirits elevated by a thought. He continues: "Everybody needs somebody for a word of encouragement. Other people want to discourage you. No matter what you're doing, they'll find some reason why you shouldn't do it. That's because they can't do it themselves, and they ain't about to let you do something they can't do. We're like a bunch of ants crawling all over, dragging each other back. One ant will get up the hill, and another will pull him back. How dare you get ahead of me!"

As the times draws closer for the bar to close, Trader, always with a smile on his face, reaches out even more compassionately to his customers. Parting, even for the night, is truly a great sorrow to him.

"Come back to see me, you hear!"

He seems to plead with his sad, moony eyes.

"If Trader died, I guess I'd grab something for a souvenir and boogie down the road," says Tex. "There'd be no reason ever to come back, with him gone."

Trader understands what Tex means. "I have my own world here. Outside the door, it's different. In here, it's just . . . well, good. I

Tex in his modified truck.

don't let the outside interfere with Trader's. I like everything out there, except it's disturbing sometimes the way people create their own downfall. They don't look to help anybody. I try to make them feel wanted in here, accepted. I tell them that they can do things, not only for themselves, but for others."

After closing, the dressing room is overtaken by the late-hour quietness. The dancers are tired, and the strain shows in their faces.

Slowly, they change into their street clothes, while Trader cleans out the cash register and goes through the motions of closing the bar.

Everyone moves in slow motion. Sentences are left unfinished.

Reality sometimes takes your breath away with much razzle-dazzle, other times it dissipates like a slow leak.

Earlier in the evening, the author and photographer broke for dinner and then visited a jewelry store to pick up mementoes for the dancers. Back at the bar, they gathered the women together and presented them with their gifts—a silver ankle bracelet with a small heart inscribed with the words, "Thanks—from Jim and Steve."

There was a moment of stunned silence, after which Lisa laughs, quickly followed by everyone except Rive, who grimaces and says, "This is it? This is the gift?"

"It's the thought that counts," says Lisa, reaching out to hug the author and photographer. Lisa's gesture quickly turned into a group hug, punctuated with hysterical laughter.

Afterward, Krystal has a surprise of her own. She embraces the other women, tears running down her cheeks.

"This is goodbye," she says. "Bush and me, we're leaving tonight."

Her voice cracks with emotion.

"Don't tell Trader. He don't know yet. I don't want him to feel hurt. Not until after we're gone."

Outside, on the rain-soaked streets, slowly walking couples and roving bands of sailors, some staggering, make their way along Palafox Street, receding into the dark—many of them optimistic about tomorrow, others dream-busted and down on their luck.

Palafox Street looking north from Trader Jon's.

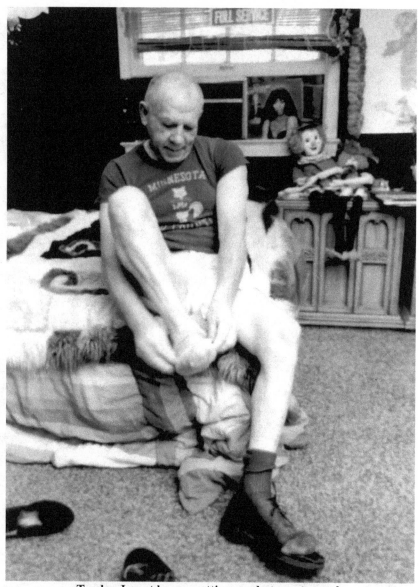

**Trader Jon at home, getting ready to go to work
by putting on his mismatched socks.**
Photo by James L. Dickerson

7

TRADER JON'S WITHOUT THE GIRLS

March 1987

Over the years, Trader Jon's has changed greatly, yet the more it changed, the more it seemed to stay the same. Gone are the doe-eyed dancers, replaced by musicians. Instead of bumps and grinds, patrons these days are greeted by wailing guitars.

"I always wanted to come back to music," Trader explains. "Blues, rock 'n' roll, jazz—but dance music mostly."

Trader's daughter, Cheri, works in the bar now, along with her husband, and although she speaks fondly of the dancers, she is glad they no longer perform at the bar.

Dancing is a high-risk occupation, yet most of the girls who danced at Trader's are still around town, with the exception of Krystal, who was never heard from again after she struck out for South America.

Cookie tends bar at a topless club across the street from Trader's.

The whereabouts of Julie and Lisa are unknown.

Rive, who wanted to go to law school, instead married a Coast Guard officer.

Life goes on as usual for Trader. Not long ago he acted as bartender for Bob Hope's television salute to naval aviation. After the show, Hope and his wife, Delores, and the Secretary of the Navy and his wife, trekked to Trader's bar for a proper salute to naval aviation.

"It was really beautiful," says Trader. "Bob Hope is an exceptional man. He's the most beloved man in the U.S.A."

In 1997 Trader Jon still had a relationship with the Navy, but it was no longer the same. Times had changed. For decades, he provided a safe haven for young sailors and aviators. With a wink, the Navy approved of Trader Jon's nightly adult entertainment.

The dancers who worked there mostly came from local neighborhoods. There were not hardcore circuit dancers with enhanced breasts. Most were of junior college age and looked and talked like the wives and girlfriends the homesick sailors and aviators left behind to serve their country. The Navy looked the other way because Trader Jon's provided a safe atmosphere for the men. Naval purists dismiss the importance of the women to Navy morale, but to do so is to deny the realities of life in the Navy.

Trader interrupts his story to sign an autograph.

A young boy, about ten, looks up at Trader with admiration as his father excitedly hands Trader a pen with which to sign his name on a non-descript piece of paper.

The boy looks at the autograph, and then back at Trader.

"Cool," the boy says.

Trader chuckles as the boy's proud father escorts him out of the bar. "I don't remember his father, but when he was in the navy he must have found something here that he needed."

As a poet, a newspaperman hiding out in the south of Florida, once wrote over a glass of beer and shared with the author only on condition of anonymity:

Trader Jon's

Home of Pensacola's finest—

and Pensacola's worst.

It is the nicotine in a billion cigarettes

And the dying ricochet of years' old laughter

bouncing round the room;

It is the talk of parachutes, pari-mutuels, prisoners of war

And victims of peace; A place of pickups and pick-me-ups;

A nostalgic ride in a barbershop chair,

Or a nose-talgic visit to Trader Jon's

Trader Jon and his wife Jackii.

8

TRADER JON PULLS ANCHOR

February 15, 2000

Trader Jon passed away at Sacred Heart Hospital at the age of eighty-four. For the past three years he had suffered from the effects of a stroke that had left him partly paralyzed and with impaired speech. Without Trader Jon's unique personality, the club had withered away to the point where it had to be closed in 1998.

Retired Vice Admiral Jack Fetterman recalls him as someone who never said anything bad about anyone. "You talk about bonding, and you talk about brotherhood, and you talk about what naval aviation was all about," he told a reporter for Associated Press. "Trader kind of provided that foundation."

Shortly after Trader Jon's death, a Pensacola law firm, Aylstock Witkin & Sasser purchased his memorabilia and donated it to the Naval Aviation Museum Foundation, which was established to fund an entity to be named the Florida Maritime Museum and Research Center. The plan calls for the museum restaurant to be named Trader Jon's and to display the memorabilia collected by Weismann.

Co-sponsoring a "Do It!" fundraising campaign for the museum was the *Pensacola News-Journal*, which encouraged private and corporate members of the community to make personal donations that would be matched by the "Do It!" partners that included the newspaper, the Gulf Power Foundation, McGuire's Irish Pub, Whitney Bank, and the Nature Trail subdivision.

The cost of the museum was projected to be $18 million, $9 million of which was required to be raised by local donors. To date, after twenty years of fundraising, less than half the funds needed have been donated for the project. That may be because of Trader Jon's reputation as a haven for young women who danced topless to provide for their children. If so, that is a shame that can only be explained by ignorance of the cultural importance of the bar and the people who worked there.

Trader Jon is an authentic American hero. He'll never make the history books, yet more than one generation of Americans touched by him has shaped the history of a nation that seldom has really ever truly understood the wellspring of its greatness.

Trader Jon understood all too well that no country has ever been brought to its knees by naked women, especially local women with troubled childhoods who needed a safe work environment. He could

**Trader Jon is embraced by a friend
who bears a striking resemblance to Lyndon Johnson**

have operated a more traditional topless club and brought in name entertainers with enhanced breasts, but the genius of his business plan was to hire hometown girls around the same age of the homesick sailors and aviators who frequented his bar seduced by the fantasy of seeing the "girl next door" naked on a stage from which young women their age offered nothing more than friendly conversation that served as a salve for their homesickness.

If American democracy falters, it will not be because of half-naked women, but because of a diseased way of thinking that is

Trader Jon cleaning photos on the wall.

devoid of history and consequences. Trader Jon so revered American history that he devoted his life to collecting the artifacts of that history, especially those remembrances associated with America's willingness to spread the gospel of its democracy throughout the world, even if it involved the sacrifice of its youth by a military that understood that democracy demands nothing less than sacrifice.

Understanding Trader Jon's place in history was the State of Florida, which placed a historic marker in front of the building that, for nearly half a century, was Trader Jon's. He never saw that marker, regrettably, but he must have known it was coming, for if there was one thing that he had plenty of, it was faith. Not so much in himself, as in *America the Bee-you-tee-ful!*

THE WOMEN

OF

TRADER JON'S

Cookie

COOKIE

Spreading a towel out across the sand, Cookie kept a watchful eye on her three-year-old son, David.

"Don't go in the water," she shouted.

She need not have worried. Dashing toward the waves, then back again before the salty fingers of Gulf water reached his feet, David had no intention of getting wet. Back and forth he went like the tiny sand crabs that darted unnoticed at his feet, never tiring.

Early in the morning the white sand beach was deserted, except for a handful of surf fishermen and the occasional jogger. Within an hour or so all that would change. Thousands of sunbathers and swimmers would descend upon the beach, breaking the rhythm of the gently falling waves with laughter and the raucous shouts of carnival-goers. Pensacola Beach is like that. Part amusement park. Part wilderness. Located on the island of Santa Rosa, less than a mile from Pensacola, the beach ranks second only to Miami among Florida tourists.

A narrow beach, studded with picturesque dunes and wild sea oats, it winds about the island, seldom ever stretching more than fifty yards in width. At the center of the island are hundreds of clapboard and sandstone shanties, all arranged in neat rows, door to door.

Cookie

Cookie at home in her Pensacola apartment

Except for an occasional deviate—like the house build in the shape of a flying saucer—all the houses are almost identical.

During the winter, the island is largely deserted. The only hangers-on being those people who live there the year around operating restaurants, taverns and motels. Not so in summer. With the arrival of the warm balmy Gulf breezes also come sun-and-fun worshipers from all over the nation. Scavengers looking for the Promised Land.

Cookie slipped off her jeans and her top. Underneath she wore a black, two-piece swim suit. Her skin was darker than it ever had been before, tanned by countless hours on the beach. This year she got an early start, going to the beach almost daily since March.

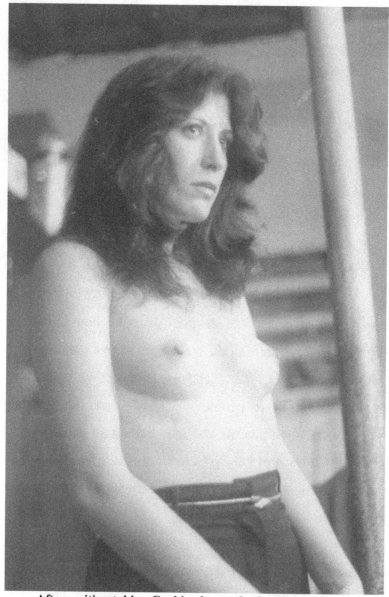

After waiting tables, Cookie pleasantly shocks patrons by removing her shirt and dancing on stage.

Cookie likes the beach. It was where she goes to do all her thinking. And in those days she had a lot to think about. Married shortly after she graduated from high school in Pensacola, her relationship with her husband had begun to deteriorate. She thought he was seeing another woman. But she just never could prove it, not even to herself, so that she could believe it with absolute certainty.

"Don't go near the water," she called out to David.

Splashing a thin layer of suntan lotion across her arms and legs, she lay across the towel. The early morning sunshine was warm. It felt pleasant against her skin. She watched David. He meant everything to her now. A scrawny, dark-headed child, he seemed precocious, ahead of many of his playmates.

Every time a fisherman or jogger went by on the beach, she looked away. If they stopped to speak, she put her head down onto her arms, ignoring them. Most of her high school friends had been female. Around men she was painfully shy. Words failed her. Not now, though. Not at Trader Jon's. Cookie, at age twenty-one, celebrated the Bicentennial basking in the sun, watching her marriage fall apart. Thinking about it. But saying next to nothing.

I was born right here in Pensacola, and my parents still live here. I've got a brother and one sister. My brother is in Miami, and my sister is in Virginia. My parents don't care about my dancing. My dad used to be a painter, but he got his shoulder messed up and he can't do too much work now. Mother works some at a telephone switchboard. My parents were strict. But I guess they weren't strict enough. My dad was strict, but my mom I could just about talk into anything.

My marriage was good until my husband got me a car. When he got me a car, I started (voice trails off) . . . . I guess it was both our faults it didn't work out.

Working at Trader Jon's is like a sponge that soaks up the loneliness in her life. I like guys who just come in and sit and talk to you without grabbing you. They know the way the game goes about the drinks, and they know what they can afford. You don't have to give them a line of shit. They know you're not hustling them.

It's embarrassing when you sit with somebody and they think you're hustling them, when really you're not because we don't make nothing off drinks. You get drunk when Trader puts anything in them, but sometimes it's just orange juice. Why should I sit with somebody I don't know and drink orange juice?

We're not making anything off them. You tell them you're not, but they don't believe you. They just think you're trying to hustle them. You don't make very good tips here, but Trader pays real good. That makes up for it. I wouldn't want to work anyplace else. If I'm going to work at night I might as well stick it out there. I'm used to the people here. If I went someplace else, I'd have to meet new people, and I wouldn't know them.

Trader's great. He lets me slide a lot. Most of the time I'm just

Cookie playing cards with her roommate Pat.

sitting around. Night before last I sat around so much I thought I was was going to get bitched at when I went to get paid. But instead he was so sweet. I don't understand him sometimes.

Nothing happened to make me stop dancing, it's just that last year I was a little wilder, and I really didn't care. But this year—and this might sound corny—but I've been thinking about my little boy. I'm just trying to raise him right, and I just don't feel like a very good mother up there dancing. I don't see anything wrong with it. But if you've got a little boy, you just can't raise him like that.

Dancing does keep you in shape, though. My titties are getting smaller. If I stop eating and lose weight, they get smaller. If somebody were to give me one wish, I'd ask for a nice ass. Yeah, give me a nice ass. That's the secret of success.

123

Lisa

LISA

The cold morning air flew into her face like a great arctic bird, smothering her with icy flutters. Hurrying along the outside passageway, she wrapped her ankle-length, flannel robe about her long, coltish legs. It did little good. The cold still crept up inside the teenager's robe and made her skin tingle.

Why am I doing this? she asked herself.

The walk from Room 121 seemed to take forever.

Just off U.S. Highway 202, between Auburn and Lewiston, Maine, the motel sat like a beacon in the night. Frequented by sports enthusiasts during the winter months, and by travelers to the state capital and to Bates College the year around, the hotel was a convenient stopover for motorists.

"The number one people pleaser," boasted the hotel's advertisements. Why not? The motel had come to represent Middle America at its cleanest and most wholesome best.

Less than a year out of Florida's Ocala State School for Girls, Lisa—at seventeen—was out on her own, making it as a slightly above-minimum-wage dancer . . . now working at a topless bar in

Lewiston.

Given a special rate at the hotel, Lisa and her girlfriend often helped out at the switchboard during off-hours. Now, at 6 a.m., she was on her way to one of the guest rooms to awaken a member of a semi-pro hockey team who had checked into the hotel a few days earlier. He had asked Lisa to awaken him early.

"Never hear the phone," he told her. "Just come on down and give me a nudge. I'll leave the door unlocked."

Florida was never this cold. It was mid-February, and the temperature was locked at near-zero. Lisa's footsteps smacked against the concrete walkway, sounding frozen, like ice.

Slender, with long, black hair that fell past her shoulders, Lisa was a striking young girl. Her skin was fair, without blemish, and her eyes, dark as virgin coal, blazed with promise.

If the time she spent in Ocala, or before that Butte Detention Center, had broken her spirit, there was no sign of it on her face. She had only finished the eighth grade before the courts sent her away, but there was nothing slow about her.

* * *

My mother was a real strict person. I couldn't shave my legs until I was a certain age. I couldn't wear makeup until I was a certain age. I had a lot of boyfriends. But I never really dated them, if you know what I mean . . . It went on that way until I finally said, look, this is the last straw. I'm going to do what I want to do. So, Mother sent

Lisa is into self defense.

me, well, she didn't send me, the judge did, to Ocala. I was there four months for running away from home and, I was working at a Burger Chef there and I came home with $400 that I had made. It was a program they just started up, and I was one of their best students. Because I wanted my independence so much I didn't care what price I had to pay to get it.

Out at Butte Harbor I was a volunteer counselor. I was about fourteen or fifteen and had been through so much. I could tell people about it, you know—what's happening. I got a lot of young guys and girls closer to their parents by just talking to them. Their parents would come out on Sunday, visitation day, and I would sit down with the parents and the child and try to explain to the parents where we were coming from, because, you know, the times were changing.

* * *

Knocking at the door, Lisa ached from the cold. She waited, but there was no answer. She wrapped her robe tighter. Then she turned the knob and slowly opened the door. It was dark inside the room.

"Gary," she whispered.

No Answer. She stepped inside, shutting the door behind her.

"Gary, wake up," she said, seeing a man asleep on the bed.

They used to play on the switchboard and call the guys up and tell them it's time to get up, all sexy like . . . and the guys would say, "What? Who is this?"

Nudging the man, Lisa leaned over the bed. He lay very still, and

Lisa doing her makeup.

she wondered if something was wrong with him.

"Gary," she said, "It's time—."

Suddenly, he had her by the arm, pulling her over into the bed.

Stop!" she cried out. "Gary, stop!"

Then he sat up, his forearm pressed against her neck, his other hand clawing beneath her robe. Lisa struggled. With her robe and gown pulled up over her waist, the man tried to touch her.

Pushing hard, she got free and tumbled off the bed to the floor. Scrambling to her feet, she dashed for the door, fleeing out into the cold, her breath hissing steamy clouds as she fled back down the walkway to her room.

There were other requests from that room, but she never went back. She was scared of him, even if he was a hockey star. He was a big guy. He would have won. He could have taken it.

"I wasn't a virgin or anything, you know," she explained. "But, still, I didn't want to have sex with him. That's my right as an American, isn't it?"

* * *

Believe it or not, I think that my boobs, small as they are, are the prettiest thing about me. At least they're shaped. They're not hanging, one over here and one over there. I guess if they hung way down on my chest, or something, and were nothing but old flab, I guess I would use silicone. For now, I'm a happy camper.

When I'm on stage I exert a lot of energy. I use every bone and muscle in my body. But I'm usually not tired when I get home. I'm usually ready for more. I just love music. I tried quitting, but I never will again. Unless I'm forced to.

I just live day to day. When I get tired of dancing, I guess I'll find something else to do. I've already done what I wanted to do. I wanted to become a dancer, and I did. I wanted to be a star in my hometown, and I am.

I told my mama when I was thirteen that I wanted to be a dancer. There was a topless go-go bar down the street.

"Mama," I said. "That's what I want to do."

"You don't want to do that."

"Uh-huh," I said.

Lisa with her daughter.

At first she didn't like it, but after a while she started making go-go costumes for me. She's been to see my show several times. She tries to give me hints on how I could be better. It's good to have a mother who understands. She tries to understand me. It's not easy, I know . . . my father died when I was real little.

I go out to these discos and I see all these women. They're always putting on a fashion show, trying to out-dress the other one, you know. They're so plastic. So phony. Hell, I go out however I feel like dressing. I just go out there and meet people and talk to them and dance with them.

I don't get lonely unless I have time on my hands. Like in the daytime, when Liz is taking a nap and nobody else is here, I sit and listen to the radio, thinking about the old times and what I'd like to be doing, which is probably making love.

I get lonely a lot, I guess.

Sometimes at Trader's I get to feeling lonely. Like I was dating this guy named Light Bear one time and he got killed on a motorcycle, and sometimes at work I still expect to see him coming through the door.

I'm a real—what do you call it?—a real daydreamer.

Like at Trader's there are people there, but they're not keeping me from being lonely. At the end of the night I start getting tired, and know I'm going home by myself. I get real lonely then. Even when I'm dancing my mind will drift. All of a sudden I'll be through dancing, and I'll say, oh . . . my body's still dancing but my mind is not into it.

It's hard not to get turned on when you're dancing with no clothes on. You've got sex on your mind all the time. You have to because you're up there showing your body and there's men sitting out there. I get aroused. Especially if the crowd's getting into it, or if there's somebody out there I want to please. I don't have orgasms though. I'm not that easy to please. I wish I was.

When I first started out I worked with a seven and a half foot boa constrictor. Once he got loose in the audience. I had him on the stage, and he was wrapped around my ankle and I kicked my foot up and when I did he let go and soared through the air and landed on a table out in the audience. They really got excited about that.

But it wasn't a problem. I went out and got him back.

Another time I was doing a rug act. I was up on the rug, and a couple of guys were sitting at a table and they just all of a sudden grabbed the rug and pulled it on top of their table.

I freaked out. I just about died I was laughing so hard. I don't get mad at the guys so long as they don't do anything they're not supposed to out of the ordinary. I just laugh about it and keep on doing what I'm doing.

Trader is like this. If you come in and do your job, OK. He'll cut up with you. He'll say, "Here, have a drink with my friend." If you're late, he'll give you one of those looks. Like don't do it again.

Lisa exercising outside her mobile home.

If you're real late, and keep doing it, he'll tell you to take the night off. In other words, if you take the night off tonight, you may not have a job tomorrow. And he doesn't like the girls drinking beer. I don't know why but he's just funny about that, even though we do.

When guys come in and flash their money and ask me to go to dinner, I tell them no, because I know what they want.

"No thanks," I say. "Put your money up. Spend it on someone else." I tell them I'm not the girl they're looking for. Usually, they'll say, "Well, who is? Do you know anybody?" Are all guys like that?

Up there on stage you feel like a star. After you start getting down to the nitty-gritty and the audience likes it, you don't feel bad at all because you know they appreciate you. You just get up there and do what you feel. Some nights I'm really crazy and get up and dance on the tables and pour beer all over me or something just to excite the guys. Even if I have to smell like beer all night at least I made them happy. That's what they're here for. They pay my salary.

I like to see a lot of smiles. But sometimes the guys can be obnoxious. A girl will be dancing and maybe she'll have a big bottom or a thick waist or fat legs.

"God," they say. "I couldn't take her nowhere. I couldn't even take her to a dog fight."

"Wait a minute," I say. "This chick is up there dancing and all you can do is bad-mouth her. But still you sit there and look at her. If you don't like the way she looks, why don't you look the other way?"

It really makes me mad because it takes a lot of nerve to get up on that stage. I just try to write it off. I try not to think about it. I have this little saying I carry around with me:

"I may not be perfect, but parts of me are excellent."

Lisa at home with her daughter.

Julie

JULIE

I used to clean houses for a living when I first got out on my own.

That was at fifteen, when I was living in Dallas.

I ended up working at a Waffle House.

When I left Dallas and came to Pensacola, Trader Jon's was the first place I walked into. He came up to me and said, "Hello—how you doing?"

I told him I was looking for a job.

He asked me if I'd like to get up on the stage and dance.

I did and he hired me on the spot.

Trader is easygoing. I've never met a better boss than him.

There was this old man who used to come in Trader's, and he had money. He always bought the girls drinks and chicken. He spent a thousand dollars a night. Well, one night his car stalled and he asked me to give him a ride home in my little Vega, but I told him the car wouldn't make it.

He says, "If your car doesn't make it, I'll buy you another one."

So I took him out to his house and he asked me if I would sleep with him.

I told him, "Hey, I'm younger than your daughter. I don't get off on doing that."

He said, "All right, all right."

So I stayed there the night. The next day I was driving back to town with him to take him to get his car and my heater hose busted. That day he bought me another car and I've still got it.

Dancers are just as sweet as anybody else. Of course, you got your rough ones. The hard core. But you find that in any type of business. My private sex life is no different than anyone else's. When I'm up on that stage, sex is the last thing I think about. I'm concentrating on my movements. Muscle control. Music. Smiling. Trying to get everybody to smile back at me. I look at this as an art form. It's not like any other job, where you have to work eight hours and go home and then back to the same old thing.

I used to ride horses back in my younger days. I won lots of ribbons and trophies. I had a Shetland named Cindy and an Arabian named Frosty. It's been seven years since I rode a horse. I was born a country girl. Listening to country and western music. Wearing western clothes and everything.

The first time I had sex, my thought was "Is that all?" It happened in Saint Angelo, my hometown. In a car. By a river. Radio on. I

don't remember the song, but I remember him shaking life a leaf. I guess he thought, "Oh, I'm getting a virgin. I'm getting a virgin!" But it didn't bother me. I guess riding horses busted my cherry. I

was pretty young, but I wanted to know what everybody was talking about. I didn't want to ask any questions. I wanted to find out on my own. So I just jumped right out there and said, "Show me!"

I got raped by bikers twice. They kidnapped me and took me to their house. Three of them. But they didn't hurt me because I wasn't fighting them off. I couldn't call the cops on them because I didn't want to get busted. And I darn sure wasn't going to get somebody to whip their ass. You just don't do that. I let it slide. I've been fortunate. Definitely.

When I'm up there dancing, I try to think about the music. I get nervous, sometimes, too nervous, and I start worrying about what the customers are thinking because I'm a very sensitive person. There are times when everybody is with you, standing up and clapping. It's the best feeling in the world. When they're not that way, though, it can be the worst feeling ever.

I've walked off that stage, just slinging costumes on the floor and stomping on them. Then I have to calm down and get everything back together. But that's not me. That's what someone told me one time. I was constantly looking for the answer about why I sometimes feel the way I do. Why do I feel bad sometimes when I get up to dance, when really I don't feel that way.

It's the vibes people are throwing at me, somebody told me. They're over dominating you. They're getting over on you. You can't let them do that. And it's hard.

Julie

Even now, I still get nervous. I can't help it.

I like customers who can look at me the way I look at them. Just easygoing people. Not expecting anything. Just watching and observing and appreciating. When somebody sits out there and sticks their tongue out, and starts talking about what they would like to do to you, I ignore those types. I don't want to hear that. They should have more respect. I am a person, too.

My mama always told me, "You *can* be a lady and dance."

Rive relaxing before she changes into costume

RIVE

I've been described by some people as the epitome of music. That means my body shows what the music feels, and I feel what the music feels. I know my songs well. All the little booms and baaas, every nook and cranny.

Taking off your clothes never really gets boring.

It's inevitable they'll come off. You know someone is watching you. They're fully clothed, but you're not. So you know they are halfway aroused, and you automatically get that way yourself. They know they can't do anything right then and there, so they approach you later, and inquire what you're doing that night.

I don't think of myself as being a sexy person. I find myself average. But then there are lots of people who will tell you that you are, so I just say, thank you. My sex life is average. Now I have it maybe four times a week. Average to most people I guess would probably be once a week. Now I'm just trying to take it easy. There's really no one here I'm ready to get involved with.

I think my bust is the part of me that's the most appealing to men.

Rive

You know an enormously big chest just doesn't look good to me.

A place like this gets boring when the room is empty. You have to sit around, and sometimes there are not enough people to talk to. What I like to see most are smiles. The audience enjoying the music, and appreciating you dancing . . . dancing to please them, and dancing to please myself. Occasionally you see them staring, and you just go over there and tease them a little bit. Usually you get a good reaction. It's a crowd pleasing business.

Dancing is a lot of good exercise. But when I go home, I do at least fifty sit-ups a night, and I do exercises for my waist and hips. It's a sort of discipline. I don't care if I'm a little tipsy. I force myself to do it. I take off my makeup every night, too. I don't sleep with makeup on.

My family's a lot different than I am. My Dad's a very strong Southern Baptist, and he doesn't approve at all of what I do. My dad was in the service, stationed in Hawaii, where he met my mom and they got married. They lived there eleven years before coming to Pensacola. Dad thinks I should do something better. But don't most fathers? You know, they have this image of their little daughter. But it's not always going to work out that way.

My parents were very strict. But I'm not rebelling, not at all. My father used to make me go to church and things like that. He was the type of person who said if you live under my roof, you do what I say. My sister thinks I'm immoral. She was hired at the navy base as a temporary helper but they kept her on. What she does, to me, is very boring. She works as a computer terminal operator.

Trader Jon is a fabulous person. I have never had any arguments with him, never disagreed with him. He's never cheated me out of money or anything. He's just an all around great person. The girls here are the same way. I haven't run across another person yet that I haven't liked. They're personable. They'll bend over backwards to help you.

I'm a very motivated person. I want to get what I want out of life because you know when you decide something and you think you really can handle it, I think you should try it. At least give it one

Lisa helps Rive get dressed.

good try. I guess that's what makes me different. What I want is so much different. Most girls want to sit around and be housewives or secretaries, nothing really too high up. I want better things out of life. They're willing to be in a rut, and do the same thing every day and not excel in life.

I'll keep dancing long as I really need to do it. I plan to stay here a few more months, and then I'm going to go back West, and then I plan to attend college in the daytime and dance at night. I'd like to be a lawyer. Something in the entertainment field. I'm trying very hard to prepare myself. Not so much for being a lawyer for dancers, but for television stars, singers, movie stars.

I want to study law because I have the drive to do it. I'm an inquisitive person anyway. It'd be easy for me to ask questions the way lawyers do. I like that type of public relations . . . being able to get people out of sticky situations.

Rive backstage.

Krystal

KRYSTAL

I graduated from the ninth grade. Tenth grade told me to go away. Seems I was a little too ornery for their liking. I'm the type of person who's sort of semi-allergic to cement. I'd rather have the earth under my feet. I'd rather be out on a farm raising my crops and raising kids.

There are lots of farms that belong to the Rainbow People, and I'm a member. At the Woodstock gathering we discovered we could put a couple thousand people together and have a good time and learn a bunch of stuff and nobody get in trouble.

OK, so we're going for it. Every year, up in the mountains, we have what's called the Rainbow Family healing gathering. What we are is a tightly-knit, loosely-organized society that wants to bring back the Native American way of life. When people from the cities hear about us, they come to our gatherings and we start de-programing what television has done to them.

Television—people who watch television fall for the Coke commercial. Coke isn't good for you. We try to show them natural ways. How to live in harmony with nature. We're scattered all over

Krystal and Bush

the place. About half of us are in Guatemala now. I hope to be in Guatemala for the major part of the winter. We're spread out more or less on the west coast, and back toward the east coast as far as Oklahoma and Montana, and down here in Florida. I'm sure everyone knows about the recent arrests here for marijuana that were immediately filed with the rebuttal of, 'Wait a minute, it's part of our religion.'

We smoke marijuana as part of our service. The pipes that were passed centuries and centuries ago were filled with red bark, but red bark now is very hard to get a hold of, so we smoke marijuana instead during our council meetings. I still smoke it for pleasure. But most of us use it basically for religious rites.

What is important to me is the preservation of our forests. Natural lands and wildlife. I've been to almost every rally against nuclear power there has been. I've helped set up three different reserves for wildlife. My brothers and sisters have been involved with a lot of things to stop the building of cement upon the land. The Rainbow Family tries to work together as much as possible to stop the destruction of nature.

Dancing comes naturally for me. I feel music with my body. Every note I can feel in a different part of my body. That's the way I move. Most of the dancers in the Midwest are in it for the money. They're no good. Ain't got no talent. I'd like to kick them off the stage. The good dancers you'll find in burlesque. I have worked burlesque quite a bit, but I always work back-up because I don't like to haul around a lot of equipment.

When I'm up there on stage, I put my heart and soul into it. Taking my clothes off, to me, is just a coincidence which involves more money. It give me more reason to do it.

The first time I ever danced was at a place called Mary's in Portland, Oregon. I walked in with this girl, Peggy, who got me into the business. I talked to the agent. He said, "OK, I got a costume here. You put it on and we'll see how you dance."

I had these five-inch heels on and I wasn't used to wearing heels, so I stumbled across the stage, wearing a G-string, T-strap, pasties and nothing else. I punched on the music. Then came my big

Krystal and Lisa backstage.

mistake. I turned and looked at the people.

"Excuse me," I said, and off the stage I went. They had to get me a little inebriated to get me involved again. Later, I did dance for the man, and he did hire me, but I felt very embarrassed.

"Wait a minute," I said. "You guys all got your clothes on. Somebody take something off and make me feel better."

For the first year I was pretty nervous about dancing. I was skeptical of everything and everybody. I took my clothes off, but I wasn't for sale. My biggest problem was how to politely tell a gentleman no, that I wouldn't go home with him. You have to do that very gently, very gently. I've always been the type who doesn't like to be fondled in public. That's not the place for it. That goes between the sheets, behind closed doors. Just because I'm from California, that doesn't mean I've been in orgies.

If a man touches me while I'm on stage, I will politely ask him not to do it. If that doesn't work I start to get uptight. If he does it again, I tell him it's a no-no, to cool it.

When you're up on that stage and they applaud for you, it makes you feel good. You just feel good all over. It's not so much taking your clothes off. That's just part of the trip, you know. It's not my actual reason for being up there. I love entertaining people.

Dancing is hard on you when you first start. My third night, I came home and sat down and my legs froze in position and I had to be carried to bed. I thought I was paralyzed. At that time I was involved in my first marriage. My husband rubbed my legs down real good, and the next day I got up and they were still sore. But at least they weren't frozen anymore.

I love working at Trader's. I don't know Trader all that well, but what I know of the man I like. I know he stands behind his girls. If somebody starts getting a little too hanky-panky and won't listen to the girl's refusal to get involved, Trader will just say, "Hey, cool your jets or out the door!" If you're one of his girls, all you have to do is call him and he'll take care of you.

A good customer is someone you can sit and talk to and not have to hustle him to get a drink. A bad customer is someone who sits in there and gives you a hard time. A good customer is someone who pays attention at least part of the time, someone who is polite and shows a touch of class.

What I tell girls just starting out is to make sure you want it.

Number two, don't cuss too much.

Number three, pick music you know.

When I first started, the people I danced for had a master of ceremonies who picked the music. I had no idea what music I'd be dancing to. That's a hard way to learn, but you learn good that way.

You never know why people come to bars like this. Some are here because they want to see someone with their clothes off. Some are here because they're lonely and they hope they'll get some attention. Some are here because they want to go partying and this is the place they do it. Some are here because they didn't have anything else to do and they were passing by. I don't know of a bad reason to be anywhere. Unless it's a prison when you're innocent.

My father is a full-blooded Chippewa. He was in the service and took voluntary station in France after serving in the Korean War. He met my mother there and married her, and from there, they went on to produce seventeen kids. I'm fourth from the bottom.

I've traveled all over the country. I'm rather a nomadic person. My first husband got me into this business after we started doing quite badly. I wanted to get my son out of the gutter, so I went to work as a dancer. My mother can't stand it. My father says everybody should so what they want to do.

THE AUTHORS

Steve Gardner, left, and James L. Dickerson
with the women of Trader Jon's

AUTHOR

Perhaps best known for his investigative biography, *Colonel Tom Parker: The Curious Life of Elvis Presley's Eccentric Manager*, which was purchased by Warner Bros. for the film *Elvis*, starring Tom Hanks as Colonel Tom Parker, James L. Dickerson is an award-winning newspaper journalist and author, originally from Greenville, Mississippi.

A longtime resident of Memphis and Nashville, he was an editorial writer for *The Commercial Appeal* and a book critic for the Nashville *Tennessean.* His Memphis-published magazine *Nine-O-One Network*, at one time the third-largest circulation music magazine in the U.S., made history by becoming the first Southern-based magazine to obtain newsstand distribution in all 50 states and overseas.

Dickerson's biography of guitar legend Scotty Moore, *That's Alright, Elvis,* co-authored with the guitar legend, was a finalist for the Gleason Award. His music history, *Mojo Triangle: Birthplace of Country, Blues, Jazz and Rock 'n' Roll,* was a first-place winner of the IPPY Award for best non-fiction book in the South. Dickerson and photographer Steve Gardner spent more than a decade getting to know Trader Jon and the women who worked there.

PHOTOGRAPHER

CPSIA information can be obtained
at www.ICGtesting.com
Printed in the USA
LVHW110450120822
725755LV00002B/39